DaYetta "Dee" Collins

D1598178

GREAT MAN WHERE ART THOU ?

The Silent Cry of a Woman's Heart ...

Dedication

It is a privilege and honor for me to dedicate this book to all the men who are in my life, and to those who have come and gone. First and foremost, I am referring to the great men in my family. I can honestly say, "The men in my family are great men; Real Awesome Men." I want to speak directly to the heart of my two oldest brothers; John Calvin Howard and Michael Keith Howard. Although, I haven't always been aware of this, you provided me so much emotional stability. As a young woman, learning life lessons, and doing my very best as a good woman, I strived to have rich relationships. Yet, on many occasions, I fell short. However, as I have gone through extensive processes of emotional healing my eyes have been opened to see you as great men. You contributed to me having a firm foundation to never give up on my dreams. You emotionally protected and loved me without any scars, wounds or tainting of what a brother was created to be; A Builder. As your baby sister, you've built me up in so many ways in order for me to be the great woman God has ordained me to be. At this tender age of 52, I am still growing and developing in a wholesome manner, because of the foundation that you laid since my birth. I am assured that I will experience so much more in life with a great man who needs me, and is willing to embrace me; love me with all my flaws, as I respect him. It is for this reason God will satisfy me with me long life. Psalm 91:16. You are my role models.

Secondly, I dedicate this book to every young woman. First and foremost my daughters, Allison and Ariel Fuller, as well as my nieces, cousins, mentees, and every spiritual daughter God entrusted in my care. Each chapter of this book was written from my heart to yours. I always desired for a great woman to teach me what they learned from their relational trials, tribulations and triumphs, so I can avoid making the same mistakes. Fortunately, this did not happen in the manner which I desired. If it did, I would not be writing this book with a hope and expectancy that it will teach you what no one taught me. To young women, it is inevitable that you learn your own life lessons. You will experience your brokenness and disappointments strictly designed to humble you. However, I don't believe that your pains should be as severe as mine due to lack of knowledge and wisdom. So, please allow this book to teach you lessons from the silent cry of my heart, so you will succeed far greater than me, as well as many other great women who have passed through this life.

Lastly, I dedicate this book to a great man, Clemont Craddock, Jr. , who afforded me the opportunity to be in his life. He exposed me to the personal and private domains of his heart and home. I am confident that he doesn't give this opportunity to just any woman, so I am honored. To me, you are a man like David who wrote Psalm 37:23 – The steps of a good man (warrior) are ordered by the Lord; and he delighteth in his way. Well, one thing I know for sure; you are a warrior. Through your experiences, unknowingly, your mindset has been trained as a Kingdom Man, which is powerful beyond measure. For God to order your steps to me simply confirms His seal on my life as a "Woman of Worship" elevated to another realm in prayer. Since the first time I heard your voice, I have been praying for you, because I felt the heart of my Heavenly Father I experience in worship. As a result, I realized that only a great woman can be trusted with your heart, because it is precious and pure in the sight of God in spite of your past pains. You have no idea how God has strengthened my heart and soul, as He has assigned me to pray, worship and spiritually war on your behalf. I'm humbly grateful. As a great man, my spiritual womb has been fortified, as I always aim to walk in the Spirit, and allow Him to reveal His predestined plans. So, I thank you for your unknowing contributions. I pray that as you continue to seek the face of God, He will bless you with the great woman assigned and divinely ordained for your life and legacy. You deserve nothing but the Love (Agape) of God that consists of kindness, patience, peace, joy and faithfulness.

Table of Contents

GREAT MAN WHERE ART THOU?

The Silent Cry of a Woman's Heart...

ACKNOWLEDGMENT

This work is the product of many God-ordained experiences. I am forever grateful to Our Father for every person He has chosen to bring into my life and every situation He has allowed me to endure. I am grateful for every man and woman who God allowed me to pastor, coach, counsel and lead from DaVetta Collins Ministries to present the day Next Level Leadership Institute & Coaching Center. Your presence and the mandate from God for me to labor with you developed me in many amazing ways.

For the development and production of this book, I am especially thankful to the dynamic power team at Dunamis Woman Media & Publishing, Inc., including the Project Administrator/ Creative Writer, Editors, and Transcribers who worked tirelessly and efficiently to produce the manuscript. Also, to the Legal and Marketing teams for ensuring that every aspect of the production process was delivered with excellence. What I appreciate the most is that you not only put your hands to war and fingers to fight, but you prayed with and for me during this extensive process.

To my friends in ministry and business, you inspire me to live out my dreams and I say, "Thank you". No one would ever believe what we all have endured on our journeys. But God! Your support, shoulder to lean on and mentorship has been key to my growth and development.

And finally, to my beautiful daughters and granddaughter, you have been with me through thick and thin, from relationship to relationship, and I am grateful for you. You are me and I am you and together we will influence future generations. You are the hope and future of our lineage!

GREAT MAN WHERE ART THOU?

The Silent Cry of a Woman's Heart...

FOREWORD

The Word of God speaks about the attributes that a virtuous woman possesses in Proverbs 31:10. Based on that description, I personally know the author of this book to be a virtuous and Dunamis Woman. She has pressed and persevered through many struggles to achieve her goals to get to this place in her life. As her sister, I watched her growth since childhood, which has been about consistently leaning and depending on the Lord. As an entrepreneur, teacher, counselor and mother, she is insightful and accomplished. She wears many hats, but it's not about "doing" for her. I believe her greatest role is in her "being" what God has graciously created; an amazing woman.

The understanding that you will find in the following pages is life changing. For the woman who believes for that relationship with a Real Awesome Man (A Great Man), or even closer relationship with God, this book will certainly assist you in the journey to discover both. You will see how even through tough times and pain, God has a specific plan for your life, and strategies in place that will lead you directly to your destiny. For the Real Awesome Man who is seeking a Dunamis (Virtuous) Woman and/or stronger relationship with God, this book will support your desire to excel in these areas. As the great man, you will learn how a broken woman can become the great woman that God has designed specifically for you.

I pray the power of the Holy Spirit aid you while reading these powerful words, so that you too will be able to help someone else find their inner strength and courage. DaVetta has been transparent in her experiences in hopes that her story will give you the tools to live a more fulfilled life.

> *"He comforts us in all our troubles so that we can comfort others when they are troubled, we will be able to give them the same comfort that God has given us"*
> **(1 Corinthians 2:4 NLT)**

– Ann Anthony

GREAT MAN WHERE ART THOU?

The Silent Cry of a Woman's Heart...

PREFACE

The heart and soul of many women are crying out. They are seeking for a great man; a man who values and loves them unconditionally. Across this country and around the world, can this cry be heard verbally? Absolutely not! It resides solely in the recesses of a woman's heart and in the seat of her deepest emotions. In the subconscious of her mind she desires to be loved, cherished and adored exclusively. One man for one woman, she doesn't want to share.

Every man and woman desires to have a trusted friend. For a woman, that friend in a man serves as a protector, provider, comforter, and leader. The Holy Spirit, the Trusted One, is an example of how these attributes aid us. Even when a woman doesn't feel His presence, He is committed to her in spite of her faults, failures and idiosyncrasies. His commitment is unfailing without fault finding. That's love –Agape love at its finest!

As a great woman, I have come to a place and point in my life that I am tired of doing everything for and by myself. Not just to "do," but having to "be" everything for myself and my children. I am adamant that emotional healing is needed for every woman. All of us have been damaged in one way or another. However, for women, like me, who have not had the privilege of experiencing a father (man) prevalent in our life, our wounds run deeper than most.

In relationships, I have been told on various occasions, "Stop playing the man and wearing the pants." I heard this from men who were in my life intimately, but were not willing to step up to the plate to sacrificially protect and provide for me. They saw me fighting, but did not step in to help. They failed to realize I was never playing the man or aspiring to do so. I just wanted them to see my wounds, pick me up, carry me off the battleground and love the hell out of me. They left me wounded and wondering, "Great Man Where Art Thou?"

Beyond needing and desiring protection and provision, especially in the area of my emotions, I have always longed for true companionship. I firmly believe that nothing can compare to a man and woman standing united; in full agreement of their mission and purpose. For a great woman, this is vital. With companionship come the benefits of affection, affirmation, and adoration without accusations. This is a pure and wholesome camaraderie between a man and woman that doesn't hold them in bondage, but allows each one to be free while walking in their authenticity and autonomy.

My silent cry remains to be free to *be* the woman God created me to <u>be</u>. Am I perfect? Absolutely not! Having a companion in your life allows you to show your imperfections and yet be loved, without being judged. I believe every woman's silent cry is "Can I find a man who will love the hell out of me, literally!" Every woman needs a man to be committed to her as a companion, confidant, and friend. In spite of what is sometimes felt or witnessed their love abounds the strongest when things are at their worst.

As great women, the absence of great men in our lives leaves us prey to all kind of enemies for misuse and abuse. I have been emotionally abused on so many levels. However, I will not stop crying out to God for His holistic provisions for my life, which includes experiencing the selfless and unconditional love of a great man. He will love me for me and not because of what I can do for him, especially in the bedroom. My cry may not be your cry, but every woman carries her own internal wailing as an expression for the great man needed for her life. I firmly believe that my experiences make me attentive to the silent cry of many women, because I hear and acknowledge my own. Yet, with my head lifted high and my heart filled with peace and joy, I still recognize the need for great men in our lives in various ways. **They are amongst us**!

As great women, we must humble and deal with ourselves in order to recognize when these men are in our midst. We have residue from our past that we must confront to avoid falling into dangerous traps. You can't conquer what you don't face. It's not okay for 80% of households to be governed by single mothers. Women have been given the grace to handle enormous responsibilities, but sometimes grace is not enough. We require the real deal! We require the grace for love to be shown to us, as women, from men with genuine hearts and minds.

I have accomplished a great deal in my life, and have lost even more due to my sacrifices, especially in relationships. Yet, my heart remains pure, as I yield my will to the will of Our Heavenly Father as He would have me to be, unconditionally loved and adored. My heart's cry is not only for me, but more so for my daughters, and granddaughter. In addition, I cry for women who have never experienced the agape love of a great man. I want this book to be a tool for you to learn life lessons that weren't taught to me concerning relationships. God appointed every man in my life, including my father, to treat me the way I didn't want to be treated. I never wanted to be abandoned, rejected, betrayed nor emotionally abused. What woman does? However, these things occurred and I use them as my stepping stones for greater success. So, please know that when you read this book you are on the clearance rack. I paid a price, through my experiences, so great women like you don't have to pay the same price, if at all possible. Choose the percentage you want discounted as you gain insight, and apply spiritual principles I learned from God; The Father, Son and Holy Spirit.

As I continue to enlighten your eyes to truth, and expose my heart, this book is for women who are ready to release the sacred domains of their heart they have been self-protecting. You can't have victory without vulnerability. I desire to connect with women across the globe willing to embark upon a journey, and dig deeper into their hearts, minds and souls in order to be transformed from good to great. You will discover that the great man is in need of the great woman just as much as she is in need of him. Through this book, you will learn the difference between a good man and a great man. You will understand the need for great men. You will know what it is to be the great woman to conquer the fears that lie deep within our souls, as we are destined for greatness.

GREAT MAN WHERE ART THOU?

The Silent Cry of a Woman's Heart...

INTRODUCTION

A s Dunamis Women, women of power, it can be very difficult to be honest and show vulnerability about our need to be affirmed, admired, and adored by a great man. Often times, this is hard when our hearts and souls have been emotionally violated from past experiences. Regardless, to be truly loved is a deep desire God placed on the inside of us, because without man we would not exist.

Before man was formed from the dust, "Woman" resided deep within his heart. God pulled her out and fashioned her exactly for him. That's why a woman longs for a great man. However, she can easily fall prey and settle for having a good man, because of her longing and silent cry to be appreciated. A great man sees the outward appearance, style and fragrance, but it doesn't take precedence over what he receives heart to heart, especially as it concerns her life and family. A great man is keen enough to look at the inward parts of her heart, like God, in spite of how she, as a woman, presents herself outwardly.

A woman yearns for a great man – a priest and king who knows how to position himself in life. In many cases, she is surrounded mostly by what I call "good men" (which I will describe later). These men are in the community, workplace, church, club, school and on the internet. A woman can devalue her self-worth and compromise her well-being by allowing this "good man" to be in her private space and environment. Does she always recognize that he is just a good man? Not really. Unfortunately, we recognize this after we have become involved, and certain circumstances have taken place such as pregnancy, marriage, abuse, infidelity, debt, etc.

In many cases, everyone, even a host of good men, including our father, brother, son, nephew, etc. pull on us and demand from us. As great women, they recognize our inner and outer strength, as well as our ability to overcome challenges thrown in our way that are usually insurmountable. As Dunamis Women, we are too busy exemplifying our power by raising children, developing in our career, continuing our education, and/or caretaking for family members and friends. Our power can become misused and abused as a result of taking on many roles and responsibilities. Without thinking about our own needs, we have a deep longing to be properly touched, held and regarded.

Unknowingly, a great woman can be captivated by a "good man" who comes her way, offering her little more than verbal acclaim for all her efforts. She can be so depleted that he can get away with diminishing her value. Because it is very rare that a man does something for her, she'll perceive menial gestures as huge. This will make her believe that she is being loved when in reality; she is only being set up to be disappointed by another good man. Her hemorrhaging emotions to be loved convinces her she's got it great, when she's only got it good. Eventually she'll discover, once again, that good is not good enough!

When it's all said and done, how much did settling truly cost her? She comes to realize that she deserves not just a good man, but a great man. Good is not good enough! Her heart continues to ache as she asks herself, "Great Man Where Art Thou?" Trying not to condemn herself, her heart continues to bleed. She silently cries deep within knowing that she is not just a good woman, but a GREAT Woman deserving better.

We, as women of power must come to a perplexing discovery that we are emotionally depleted. As a result, we are steadily fighting against guilt, shame and doubt, along with many other feelings that produce emotional anguish and pain. With our souls exposed, we still find the strength to give of ourselves. The silent cry of our hearts is that we, as women, have nothing more to give to the "good men" in our lives who attempts to suck us dry; mentally, financially, spiritually, sexually, and physically. Great men are needed to replenish us. Great Man Where Art Thou?

GREAT MAN WHERE ART THOU?

The Silent Cry of a Woman's Heart...

AGE: 57
STATUS: DIVORCED
RESIDE: AUSTELL, GEORGIA

As a man, I believe every man can define himself how he wants. A bum on the street can define himself as the finest thing since Kellogg's Corn Flakes. A guy who pays child support, but doesn't visit his kids, can define himself as a great dad because he sends a check. A guy who might show up once a month to see his kids may define himself as a great dad. Or perhaps a guy who works a job every day might define himself as a great person, but yet and still he sleeps with everyone in and outside of Corporate America. A pimp on the street who's using women might define himself as a great man. For instance, a guy, who was much older than me, said to me, "Man, you know I got more hoes than clothes." I'm like "Wow, really? He told me he was 77 years old.

A person will define a great man based on his or her mindset. Some people look at religious leaders as great men. In some instances, they're more pimps in the pulpit than on the corners. Some people look at politicians as great men, but I believe some of the biggest crooks in the world hold those positions. They are white collar thieves- some of them get caught, while others don't. Some people look at social, political and community activists as great men. However, some have had children out of wedlock, cheated on their wives, and been arrested, not just for civil rights, but for other crimes and infractions. A professional athlete can be looked at as a great man for his athletic ability, but that doesn't necessarily define him as a great man. There are so many things a person can look at, so it's based upon the individual's perspective. Your perception of a great man is the view you see through your own lenses, and not what others make it out to be.

There's nothing in America that can't be individualized. As far as where are the great men, no one can say for sure. How do you define a great man? The only one I know is Jesus. I've never met Him, but in my heart He's idolized. I was raised to believe in Him. As a great man, He healed the sick, freed the bound, and He's a legend in most men's mind. From my perspective, He's the only great man that I've heard about. I hope to get myself right spiritually, so I can meet Him one day. If I stay the way I am, I don't think that's going to happen. Hopefully, we'll have an interaction at some point that will completely change my life. On earth, when it comes to finding great men, I don't know where they are. I've met people who want to call themselves great, but again, that's based upon their own perspective.

One life lesson that I would give to a woman is to believe and trust in herself for self-sufficiency without solely depending upon a man. I have a daughter, and I will tell any woman what I have told her, "When you give up all of your emotions and ability to think for yourself, and become dependent on somebody to take care of you; at that point you've given up your liberation. You're not independent anymore because you've lost yourself. You always have to know who you are as a person and a woman. As long as you know who you are; you never really give that part of yourself away to anybody. You could give your heart and love, but you never give your soul."

I took my responsibilities as a father seriously is because growing up I was raised without mine. I heard a lot of people talk about him, but I didn't know him. I never met the man until later in life. As a young man I said, "If I ever have a child he or she would know who I am." I knew as long as God kept breath in my body, I would make myself available to them and to have a role in their lives.

I am a father and no matter how minute the task or responsibility, they would know that I'm there. If they need me, I'm only a phone call away. By whatever means they choose to interact with me, I am there for them. I personally believe if a man can lie down and make a child, he needs to take care of him or her.

As a man, I didn't know how to handle a broken heart because I didn't know what a broken heart was like. I was in denial about allowing anyone to get to my heart, and I wouldn't give it to a woman. As a result, I told them lies like; "You got my heart, and I love you!" I didn't mean any of it. As I learned more about life, I became more compassionate. I was able to empathize and show more emotions. At one point, I had cut all emotions. They didn't exist. For me, a broken heart came after my daughter was born. In order to love her, I had to open up my heart; something that I always kept locked away. Raising my daughter by myself, I couldn't do so without giving my heart to her. She had to be able to feel my emotions. You can say whatever you want, kids can feel if you love them or not. I needed to learn how with cuddle her, hold her, talk to her, even cry with her and show my feelings. If I didn't have an open heart, I couldn't do that for her.

As a man, when I opened up it made me vulnerable. I allowed other people to see that side of me, which I kept locked away all my life. Whenever I did get hurt, it was because I was trying to help somebody, and give something that I didn't have myself. To tell you the truth, I didn't even know my heart was broken until I found myself really reminiscing and thinking about everything. Although, I didn't know what it was; it was an ugly and nasty feeling. I had revengeful thoughts, and a very retaliatory type attitude. I had a withdrawing type of demeanor, pulling away from everybody and blaming myself for allowing it to happen. At some point, I had to sit back and say, "Welcome to life, suck it up, get over it and keep on moving." Basically, I handled it by just learning to absorb the pain.

Chapter One

IT BEGINS WITH DADDY

I am so glad you have decided to read this book. I am confident that as you journey through these pages, the outcome will be life changing. As a Spiritual Leader, Mentor, and Coach, God has gifted me to proclaim and teach the truth in revolutionary ways that sets people free when they embrace it. I am grateful! I pray that your mind and heart are open to discover a greater dimension of your purpose, and the power you possess.

As you continue to read, I need you to understand: ALL of us are great! We have to believe this despite how we feel or what we think, and in spite of what we have (or have not) done. It's time to live victoriously, and this book will help you begin another aspect of your journey. The biggest indicator and confirmation of your greatness is that you are still standing in the midst of everything you have been through! I'm going to challenge your thinking a little further by telling you, "Your greatness does not lie within your wonderful attributes and accomplishments, but it is in your pains, victimizations, deficits and weaknesses."

Most people are afraid of the term "great" because they feel like they're boasting when speaking about themselves that way. However, greatness is about humility, confidence and assurance. Greatness is when you've endured the unimaginable and are still standing. Not only are you standing, but are still able to love and serve others with kindness and courage. As great women, we do this with our children, as well as within our homes, and communities. We do it with our mates, and in preparation for those to come. Perilous times are in the earth like never before, and it is time for greatness to stand strong in the lives of every man and woman. Greatness is not something we do it is simply "who we are!"

It's really amazing to hear many talking about how they need a good man or a good woman. However, we fail to realize that greatness is walking amongst us. In reality, greatness begins with our fathers. If it was not for the sperm of our fathers, encountering the egg of our mothers, we would not be here today. In spite of their deficits, shortcomings or absence in our lives, our fathers are the main contributing factor to our greatness. In many cases, we have been conditioned to look at the mother as the main source, and we claim siblings and family based on the mother's contribution.

It is the father's bloodline that provides the lineage no matter what. He carries the blood. It is his mind and heart that makes us connected. This is why the absence of fathers causes so much damage in the homes and has a profound impact on the community. Their role and position is vital, critical and needed. Therefore, we can't just dismiss them.

I grew up in a home with just my mother. I never learned how to fully regard, love or admire my father for who he was as a great man. When I look in the mirror, deep down in my heart, I know I am so much like him. Not just from a standpoint of greatness, but I am conquering the same deficits and unresolved issues because of it. I Am… A Great Woman.

A great woman is aware of her unresolved conflicts and issues that needs to be addressed as she continuously evolves. This makes her more than a conqueror. The core of her struggle stems from her father being in her life or lack thereof. The manifestation of her greatness is not in what she accomplishes neither are they solely in her strengths. It is within her deep pains that makes her dreams become a reality.

I look at how my father was not prevalent, which causes my abandonment issues to still surface from time to time. At an early age, I wanted to receive affection and regard from men, which caused me to settle for those who were <u>doing</u> good as opposed to <u>being</u> great. His absence made me wanted to be loved even the more. I wanted to hear the hearts of great men, especially my father's heart. He was a quiet man who did not give me his heart, as I required, because of his brokenness and pain. Although his presence was sporadic, I became acquainted with his grief stemming from what he probably did not receive by being in love with my mother, as a great woman. I wanted so much from my father, and I was searching for it in all the wrong places.

Thus far the healing I've undergone from abandonment and rejection has launched me into a great place of understanding my true self and identity. It is in those places of our lives that we are exalted and where everyone else put us down.

I thank God for my father lying down with my mother which brought me to this earth. I thank God for every man who lied down with me, cursed me out, verbally and emotionally abused me. I thank God for every man who put his hands on me, rejected me, and determined just by looking at me that he didn't like me. I truly believe that every rejection I experienced preserved me from situations that would have caused me more emotional abuse. What I lived through has caused me to soar.

The pain from my father not emotionally contributing to my life is the main ingredient that helped me develop into a great woman. For those like me, we must understand that rejection is preservation. Trust me it's the truth. I did not see it this way in the beginning. I have learned to embrace it as my reality in order to utilize it for God's given vision and mission for my life. Often times, we think our downfalls are at the hand of other people, but it is really in how we view life's circumstances. We have to stop allowing the enemy to deceive us and use feelings of rejection and abandonment against us. We must turn our past pains and circumstances around for our greatness. No matter what, we have to make a choice to come out of the state of being a victim, and live our lives to the fullest. We were fearfully and wonderfully made by the sperm of our fathers; who are great men whether they realize it or not.

Great men must fulfill their rightful places in the earth. We need them in position for current and future generations to excel in ways beyond what we have accomplished. We have to pray and ask God to reveal to us His predestined plans in order for the great men in our lives to be restored. Without them, we are damaged goods with significant voids. As great women, most of us have had unfavorable experiences due to the absence of our father's presence. This has contributed to our abuse, rejection and abandonment. I also acknowledge that men have suffered as well. I don't make light of this, yet I can only speak from a woman's perspective concerning how we have been severely damaged.

The trauma and tragedy of absentee fathers does not dismiss the fact that sperm was released in the womb of a woman to birth sons and/or daughters who are powerful beyond measure. When we fully embrace this truth about ourselves, it will literally change our lives, because it changes our perspective. It is all a part of our growth and development. No one comes out the womb displaying greatness. It is a process that is often times painful, because it is a part of our authentic self that has been hidden. This truth is revealed for self-awareness for us to make different decisions intended to take us to our destiny.

It is inevitable that women will attract men with the attributes of their fathers, even if they don't know them. The same goes for men; they will attract women with the attributes of their mothers. This revelation confirms that the men and women we encounter are only extensions of us. The mystery comes in knowing what part of you has been attracted, at what time and for what purpose. The scripture Proverbs 18:22 comes to mind which talks about a man who finds a wife (woman), finds a good thing and obtains favor from the Lord. That "good thing" literally means he finds himself. There are times this concept is hard to embrace because of all the hell we go through. It is relevant to who we are and is neither related to being good nor great.

If your biological father was not in your life, it never deterred the plan of Our Heavenly Father; who has NEVER left or forsaken you. Think about it this way; if your biological father was absent or sporadic in your life, there was something God did not want you to experience. This is not always negative or traumatic. For example, I believe that if my father was present consistently, I would have never had the struggles and challenges I experienced. Consequently, I would have never discovered the depth of my greatness inside of me. It is possible that a father can overcompensate in his giving, especially with his daughters, which hinders the process of growth. Overcompensation is ideal for masking pain. It doesn't remove it, just delays it. Everyone in this life will experience pain; it is just a matter of when and how. But God knows best!

Getting to the core of greatness brings up residue along the way. At some point, the evil seems to outweigh the good; but our hearts house all of it together. So many relationships become broken because we don't understand this mystery. In the beginning, we primarily see and focus on the goo goo eyes and lovey dovey romantic feelings, but when we really get down to the nitty gritty there is something much deeper- **our issues**! The key for wholesome relationships is to give our damaged places to God for healing. We must become healed, but then also learn how to bring healing to each other's hearts as well. Healing should transcend beyond our current relationships to produce a legacy of wholeness that remains for the prosperity of future generations.

Great woman, you are a life giver. Therefore, it is imperative that you pursue healing in your heart and soul at all cost. Whatever you have experienced in life, you are still here! Whatever did or did not happen, you are still here! With all that you are feeling, you are still here; and healing is calling you forth. Healing is waiting for you…you don't have to wait on it. You cannot be healed without first looking in the mirror. Many women have not experienced emotional healing because of pride, pity and the "woe is me" mindset. The pain was for the purpose of bringing forth your power (dunamis) to continuously produce miracles. God wants you to experience greatness in your own life, as you impact others so that they can also be healed.

One of the first things you have to do to experience all the freedom that God has for you, is to truthfully admit where you are. I had to admit that I was emotionally dead, even though at the time I was married with two beautiful daughters, living in wonderful home in a suburban community. My children had everything they could possibly want tangibly. I had the right look, all the latest fashions for me and my daughters. In church, I counseled others; and was passionate about prayer, praise & worship. It seemed as though we had it all together. However, there came a time when I could no longer keep the façade and wear the mask to please others. I could no longer smile on the outside ignoring the turmoil that was going on deep inside of me. I finally had to sit back and take a long, and honest look at me, as well as my surroundings. I was not really living, but merely existing. This assessment was for me – not my family, not my pastor, not my friends, not my husband, and not even God.

The process began for me one Sunday morning when I decided to stay home from church, which was not my custom. The situation had become just that critical for me, and I had to do something different. I had to take the time to be still, with no one but myself. I saw how dead my soul had become, and I asked God to show me "how to" become alive again. I had no idea of what that would entail, and the process was very painful, more painful than anything I had ever experienced, including childbirth. I had to decide, "Do I want the pain of change, or the pain of remaining the same?" Change is a forever process. The more that we change, the more that is required. I'm forever grateful, because my decision to change brought me back to life.

I can honestly say that emotional healing is necessary for everyone, especially women. I hold no hate or ill will towards any of the men who have hurt me. It is only by the grace of God and His healing virtue that I have learned how to truly love those who have ever misused, disappointed and betrayed me. Who teaches us how to embrace our pain? The world teaches us to get revenge and find other methods to regain happiness and comfort. We are taught to focus only on what makes us feel good. No one enjoys pain; you won't find someone in the hospital saying, "I'm glad for this pain, so don't help me." We shouldn't enjoy the anguish.

As great women we have to grasp that our pain was designed so that our power can be ignited for our family and legacy to live. It required me to realize and understand that what I had ever witnessed and experienced was for my purpose and destiny. This paradigm shift not only changed my perspective, but it changed my life. Every man who was ever in my life, beginning with my father, has contributed to my healing, deliverance, and freedom, which is a discovery to become whole. It is a beautiful thing to be able to embrace misery and distress, as tools for power building. With these tools, we can do exploits in the earth because of who we are on the inside! The truth remains that pain is housed with everything else that makes us great.

One of my favorite movies is "The Lion King." The first time I watched it, I questioned and wondered why Mufasa had to die. Simba was just a little cub when this evil came against him at the hand of his uncle. Since birth, Simba was being trained to be a king to continue his father's legacy. It was a tragedy to lose his father at the early stage of his life cycle and development. This was a sad mystery to me, but the more I watched the movie; I began to see the plan. Simba was put in a position and place to deal with his guilt and grief while learning the lifestyle of creatures considered less than. They knew their greatness with contentment.

It was them who taught him how to change his thinking in spite of his circumstances. A monkey knocked him upside the head, so that he could remember who he was and take a deep look within his soul. This was essential before Simba could be elevated to his place of royalty, rule and dominion.

The best part of the movie, in my opinion, is when his father, Mufasa, appeared to him in a vision and spoke one line, *"Know who you are!"* He did not counsel or encourage him in anyway. He simply affirmed him by proclaiming his true self and identity. But even before getting to this place in his life, he already had a lioness (great woman), Nala; who challenged his thinking enough to help him understand that he was needed in his rightful place. Without his occupancy as the king, the kingdom was a place of famine filled with pain and grief. Even this animated movie supports the main theme: It Begins with Daddy! No matter how much we try to get away from it, "Daddy" matters! You must *"Know who you are!"*

Now, I know that DaVetta is a great woman, because of my father, David Andrews. I thank God for every man who has come into my life. It is through them that I have discovered my self-worth, and it began with my Daddy. However, my true identity and destiny rest in the hand of Our Heavenly Father.

GREAT MAN WHERE ART THOU?
The Silent Cry of a Woman's Heart...

Age: 48
Status: Divorced
Reside: South Holland, Illinois

Great men are so humble that you may miss us. We are at times unappreciated and overlooked. Sometimes, we tend to be invisible because we don't have to show off; we just do our deeds every day. Just go to a school for a report card pickup, and you will see the daddies asking how their kids are doing. Or, take a walk in the park during the summer and watch dads play with their kids. Go stand on the bus line and notice the number of men drivers. Pay attention to the men who are construction workers, policemen, firemen and garbage men. Celebrate the men who grind with minimum wage jobs who are supporting their families, because those are definitely great men. We live in a world where people get fixated on status and circumstances, especially for African American men. If we don't have a ball in our hands, or a microphone-are we less than? Moreover, when bad choices are made we are vilified. Each of us has our assets and our liabilities. What I don't like to see is a woman who feels she can change a man or make him better. Although he shows her over and over again a lot of work needs to be done in him, make no mistake about, the great men are here.

I am a divorced man with a teenage daughter. I put in a lot of time and effort to have an appropriate and stable co-parenting relationship with my ex-wife. We have some good days, and there are a whole lot that aren't good. This hurts me, because I am a good dad who is treated horribly. However, I know some guys who are very challenging, yet are treated like gold by their children's mothers. I want to share a message with women, "When a man shows you that he is decent, stable, and secure: HOLD ON TO HIM!!!" You may have to go through frogs to get to one prince. So, when a man shows you how good he can be to you, know that you're worthy of receiving it.

Even with the struggles I have with my daughter's mother, I wholeheartedly embrace my responsibilities as a father. I do it to break a horrible tradition and vicious cycle. I know men and women who grew up fatherless, and I myself can remember not having my dad in my life. Because of this, I always felt that I was only half, not whole. Although my mom tried to wear both hats, she just couldn't effectively. It's impossible! As a woman, she taught me much about being a good person, but I had to seek out men, even as a young boy to fill in the blanks of my father's absence. I always made a promise to myself that if I ever became a father, my child would never experience what I felt growing up without a dad. I know I've done a wonderful job so far.

Both, the lack of a father and a failed marriage caused me heartbreak. As a man, but also as a social worker I have learned to handle it by understanding the power of healing. One of the main things to know about healing is that there are no shortcuts. You have to go through your process, and sometimes it feels like hell. For example, grief is involved with loss of any kind; including relationships. There are five stages of grief, which include: bargaining, denial, depression, anger and acceptance. There is no pass on any of the five, and the pain in your heart may initially seem unbearable. However, you're much stronger and wiser having gone through the process. The stages are not always in order: You could get acceptance, which is last, and relapse based on a memory or something and end up back at anger. Each man's journey is his alone. One may recover in a week, while another may take five years depending on where his heart was invested.

When I got divorced almost three and a half years ago, it was a year before I could even go on a date with someone else. Even to this day, I have promised myself that I am not going to get into a full term relationship until my daughter is at least a junior in high school, or possibly after she graduates. My daughter is my priority. I am responsible for her being in this world, and made a covenant with God that I would take care of her until she become an adult. I think some men forget about this pledge, because they are so focused on getting their own needs met. When I am in a relationship I give 100%. Right now, that goes to my daughter…she deserves it.

When my daughter is grown and gone, then my new chapter will begin. At that point, I can give the great woman in my life all of me. Honestly, right now all she would be dealing with is all the bitter things my ex-wife does towards me and my daughter, and how I have to be a hero for my child. That is not fair for any woman who desires a thriving relationship. I'm dealing with too much baggage right now. Most times I don't want to tackle it, but we, as men must do ourselves a favor and heal totally.

Chapter Two

GOOD IS NOT GOOD ENOUGH

I believe that everyone has the ability to display attributes that deem us as a good man or woman. However, in the era of time we are living in good is not good enough. It's time to be great! We all want greatness, but do we see ourselves as great as we REALLY are based upon our creation by Our Creator? We are all on a quest toward greatness, and now is the time and season for it to manifest according to our true origin. Everyone was born with the potential to achieve greatness. It must constantly be pursued with a relentless drive, as it relates to our respective journey.

What is greatness? Greatness is joy and happiness that comes through actualizing all the potential that God placed inside of you. Greatness is being in love with God, loving yourself, and loving those who surround you. This love must be expressed through your actions at all times in spite of how you feel. Greatness must always be sought after, and is not predicated on anyone else. Great don't wait! Greatness is always pursuing a purpose for effective living to impact and make a difference in the lives of others. But, it cannot be obtained alone.

Unfortunately, during the course of life as we pursue greatness we can become stagnant. We may encounter circumstances (e.g. financial and familial) that have accumulated over a long period of time and we don't always know how to respond. These serve as barriers while on our road to fulfilling our potential. We may find ourselves desiring someone to partner with as we are achieving our personal and professional goals. If we're not cognizant of our own purpose, we can find ourselves intertwined with someone who believes that good is good enough. In part, this explains why we have so many broken relationships and why we have a tendency to jump from person to person. In today's society, we change mates like we change shoes, every season. In avoidance, of this pattern, we must understand the precise purpose for cultivating partnerships.

We conceive the possibilities for our lives only according to how we perceive ourselves, as well as our environment. If we don't see things realistically, our perception of ourselves and others will become impaired. If a man or woman is pursuing greatness and the other is not, it is inevitable that they are going to separate in spite of love. Love is good, but not always enough. Far too many women and men stay in relationships "for love" with a person who is stuck on good and not pursuing great. That's heartbreaking and damaging.

Believe it or not, there is a difference between good and great. It's a thin line. To prevent falling continuously into pitfalls in relationships, we must know the difference in the mindsets of men versus women. Knowing the distinctive roles we both play in relationships is vital. Based upon my life experiences, it is my goal to empower you to gain more insight as you continue your life's journey.

THE MINDSET OF A GOOD MAN

The good man may present himself like a great man on the surface. Initially, it can be tricky to spot the difference. At first, a good man may endeavor to please a woman with material gains and pleasurable activities. So beware! It is easy to see so much potential in a good man, so a woman will begin to help him when he hasn't even begun to help himself. He speaks and lives only through his potential, never putting his focus on following his purpose and mission in life. Part of this may be due to him having women, including his mother, constantly at his rescue. Each time they've intervened in matters of his life, unknowingly they interrupted his internal growth and developmental process to get to the next level. As a result, he has come to expect handouts from women and has developed a sense of entitlement.

The good man enjoys what a woman does TO him. He is quite easily seduced through his physical senses and does not possess a strong will. The good man prefers not to think. He prefers not to have to use his mind too much, but he will use his penis at any time. In our society, this has become an epidemic. He thinks from the head of his penis, as opposed to his great mind. He seeks immediate gratification and a quick fix to his life's problems. Because his mindset is limited to living for today, he does not accomplish long-term goals. The relationship of convenience evolves into a routine of sex, meals, and paying bills.

The good man falters in response to life's challenges, which hinders him from being developed. What he fails to realize is that challenges are divinely designed to grow him up from the inside out in order to develop his faith. The man was created to be the anchor and the foundation. The enemy deceives a good man to think that a woman is equipped to handle his weight and occupy his place on earth. Therefore, a good man will view a self-sufficient woman with material and monetary gain as having the ability to carry and sustain him. Not so! For example, envision a woman putting a man on her back and carrying him around the room. How long do you think she will last? This inhibits him from walking through his own process towards greatness. A man is a protector and provider, who carries his own weight, with authority.

Material possessions can entice most good men and draw them into the presence of a woman. In spite of men in today's society struggling to obtain self-sufficiency, we all must remain submitted to the order of God, which will never change (I Corinthians 11:3). A good man does not understand that a woman is beautifully and wonderfully made with a tender heart that he must cultivate. As a result, the women in his life are typically emotionally depleted and drained, which can cause him to go from one relationship to another.

THE MINDSET OF GREAT MAN

A great man does things intentionally. He understands that he must be a man of character. His life impacts not only himself, but others, particularly the woman he brings into his personal domains. A great man says to himself, *"To have a great woman I must protect her in every area of her life. As a provider, it's going to cost me, not only financially, but my life is invested in her care."* He is willing to protect and provide for her with his whole heart, because he understands that he possesses what is required of him to do so. A great man brings emotional stability, mental clarity, and spiritual security because that's who God created him to be.

A great man doesn't have to try to be faithful. His vision and mission for life makes him dedicated to his great woman. A great man can look at a woman and acknowledge her beauty, and that she is wonderful, pretty and attractive to his sight. However, he doesn't allow himself to get caught up in her looks or be seduced by her flattering words that could jeopardize his legacy. A great man doesn't look to a great woman for what kind of car she drives, or how much money she makes although she is well-maintained. With humility, a great man understands that she is needed in his life.

A great man understands his need for a great woman who can handle his trials and challenges with grace. A great man admires a woman who complements his dreams and visions based upon her own. He incorporates her gifts, talents, wisdom and innate abilities to his life matters and mission. He views her as an asset not a liability. A great man's value cannot be measured monetarily. Primarily, he is great because of the wealth of knowledge that resides within his mind. A great man takes his problems, as well as the problems that arrest others around him, and creates solutions.

The mindset of a great man affords him to stand in his own identity. He does not compare himself to other men. A great man would rather remain alone instead of compromising himself to fit into the lifestyle of anyone else for mere acceptance. He stands with confidence, and will not let anyone sway him, especially the woman in his life.

I learned of these attributes of a great man when I was in the midst of my father. His absence in the home made this more prevalent in my heart. The times I was in his presence he treated me like a great woman, even as a daughter. My void and deficit ignited my ability to see his heart far beyond what he was able to give me. The longing that I have for a great man in my life is because of him. It doesn't require a lot of time to become accustom to a great man in your midst. Each time he is in your presence your heart will be impacted and an impression will be made that can never be erased.

Longing for a great man like my father caused me to learn of Our Heavenly Father. He looks beyond my faults, and He loves me in spite of my idiosyncrasies. It is this kind of love that keeps me longing for His presence, which cultivates my worship. Like Our Heavenly Father, a great man recognizes your worth, not your wealth. He sees your heart, not your home. He sees your kindness, not your kinfolk. He beholds your internal treasures; loyalty, gentleness, temperance, patience, meekness, and endurance. These great qualities within us must be proven over a period of time to the great man with intent, because his heart and mind is guided by Our Heavenly Father.

When the heart of the great man is tested by fire and he has demonstrated faith, trust and total submission, the Lord God will present the great woman to him, just as He did in the very beginning (Genesis 2:22). At the appointed time, the great man will encounter his great woman who will help him conceive all that he perceives. Unbeknownst to him, his own silent cry is being answered when he encounters the great woman. She has also been working relentlessly on her own vision, which aligns with what he's already perceived in his heart and mind.

Before we continue, let's take a minute to do a brief self-examination. God wants every man and woman healed in their souls (minds and emotions) in order for them to do His will. This requires time to reflect in some areas of your life that may have been overlooked. It is okay. I want your heart to be comforted by finding a safe place to reflect. So let your journey begin, as you walk in TRUTH by answering the following questions:

Identify at least three (3) areas in your life where you have become depleted.

_____

_____

_____

_____

Identify at least three (3) great men/women who are in your life.

_____

_____

_____

_____

Identify at least three (3) great men/women who are in your life. Based upon what you have read explain what makes each one great.

_____

_____

_____

_____

Identify at least three (3) ways that you may have settled and/or compromised your standards, based upon what you have read thus far.

_____

_____

_____

_____

Identify at least three (3) ways you have given your heart expecting to be loved and adored.

_____

_____

_____

_____

As I esteem every great woman, let me speak directly to your heart, because you have been divinely endowed with a power (dunamis) and strength beyond comprehension. It is no longer acceptable to give in to just a good man and settle for potential and possibilities. Good is not good enough! So let your hearts cry out: Great Man Where Art Thou? Stand up in who you were created to be and proclaim to the earth – I AM A… Dunamis Woman – "I am a woman who ignites my power daily to get results in every aspect of life."

Every dunamis woman needs a great man. This is necessary because his purpose is correlated to hers. For this cause God is committed to require him to live by his primary character traits; integrity and truth.

GREAT MAN WHERE ART THOU?

The Silent Cry of a Woman's Heart...

AGE: 72
STATUS: MARRIED
RESIDE: PARK FOREST, ILLINOIS

I have been married for 38 years. As you can imagine, much has been learned, taught, endured and seen within that time. When I think about the great men in this era of time (especially in our African American communities), I am hard-pressed; and not able to just roll a list from my mind. I don't recognize the "Martin Luther Kings" or the "Thurgood Marshalls." This is not because the potential is not there; however, what is lacking is humility. Many men who could be groomed and nurtured to greatness lack the understanding of the deep and abiding need for Christ. They are consumed by their own abilities and thought processes about who they are and what they can do. Some men feel like they don't need Jesus. The first step to being a great man is to accept and acknowledge Christ in our everyday living. We need the counsel and guidance of the Holy Spirit daily. Without this, we are not able to honor commitments to ourselves, let alone other relationships. This is an enormous lack for men.

The two most profound relationships that are affected by this void are the relationship between a man and his wife (or woman); and the relationship he has with his children. One of the most impactful lessons I want to share with women is to be an equal partner in the marriage or relationship. A woman cannot be submissive to the man she has to take by the hand and lead. History shows a myriad of men have had great women by their sides who have been an inspiration, a counselor, mentor, accountant and a sounding board. She has been very instrumental in his life, and insightful. Yet, he seldom gives her the credit she deserves for being his partner in life. In today's society it seems that the black woman is doing magnificent things, but there are fewer black men fulfilling roles of leadership.

One area this is very prevalent is in the home. The majority of our black youth are now being raised by single mothers. Our children are lacking leadership, love, compassion and understanding that fatherhood provides for them. This is vital not only for the young men, but the young women as well. Being grounded in Christ also establishes a firm foundation for men to learn how to be better fathers. I believe a lot of fathers do love their children, but they are not showing it. At times, it has to be an extreme situation for the fathers to come and show it.

I grew up without my father, which is one of several reasons I took fatherhood very seriously with my own kids. My stepfather was there, but he wasn't really present or active in my life until years later. I wanted to make sure mine grew up with that sense of security, and foundation of love. It shouldn't matter whether the mother and father are together or not, the children should not suffer, because of the deficits. Some men allow their broken hearts, with the mother of the children, to stifle nourishing relationships with their sons and daughters.

I am married to the mother of my children; and even though we've been together for as long as we have; I experienced a broken heart prior to her. What I believe is that you can't recover from a wounded heart by yourself. It takes an inner peace that only comes from God. He tells us in His word, if we trust in Him, He will mend that broken heart. It may take years to overcome, but you realize the fact that life goes on; and you must still live for yourself. The reality is that people break our hearts daily, and we can't allow the hurt and bruises to fester. We must ask Christ to step in. We don't want animosity to set in and make us bitter; the love of God will allow those feelings to dissipate.

Chapter Three

Genesis 12:1-2 *Now the Lord had said unto Abram, Get thee out of thy country, and from thy kindred, and from thy father's house, unto a land that I will shew thee; And I will make of thee a great nation, and I will bless thee, and make thy name great; and thou shalt be a blessing.*

For a little over a decade, I have been given the privilege of teaching great men and women spiritual principles from a biblical perspective. Personally, I have applied these teachings to my life, and so have other men and women who aspired to learn for self-application. For the purposes of reading this book you do not need to be a bible scholar. You only need to be a man or woman who desires to journey from good to great in your relationships. Please don't limit this content to a husband and wife scenario. However, I am going to begin with one of the first stories in the bible of a man and woman working together to journey from good to great; the story of Abraham and Sarah.

Every great man has an Abrahamic mantle on his life, because they are descendants of Abraham. However, God called Abram, who at that time was a good man. He made a covenant with a good man in order to take him through processes to become a great man. A great man doesn't become great overnight. He goes through a process. The first step was for Abram to make a decision to obey God without hesitation.

As a good man, the first thing God admonished Abram to do was to leave his country and family; kinfolks who thought and acted like him. Abram had to get away from his father's house so his mind could be renewed like unto his Heavenly Father. God's goal was to make his name great throughout the earth. The great man is more respected when his name is recognizable amongst others. This is a principle that will never change. His name had to change to elevate the great woman, Sarai, into her rightful place. She had to be prepared to birth great men in the earth to be positioned as kings.

The country that Abram resided in was full of grief, which he internalized. His father, Terah loss his son, Haran. He died in the land of his nativity (Genesis 11:28). Terah took his wife, along with Haran's son, Lot, as well as his other grandchildren to the land of Canaan. Not only was Abram's father filled with grief, but he was led to a place of grief called "Haran." This was the *same name* of his deceased son. God changed Abram's name to Abraham for it to become "MEGA" (great). Based upon Abram's obedience, God created new beginnings for his descendants to have a path for greatness and walk in their covenant agreement.

No longer could Abram be classified, as just as a good man who took on a wife to live by the mindset of his past. Abram had to find his rightful place with his Heavenly Father, the Creator of all mankind, in order to become the father of many nations – great men. However, he could not become a father without the womb of a great woman.

Like Abraham, the great man is not just a father to his own children, but a father to many. A father produces not mere sons from his own loins, but kings within communities and nations (Genesis 17:6). When a great man has gone through his processes of test and trials, broken only that he may be blessed, then God steps in and changes his whole life to give him dominion in the earth.

The great man can't produce a nation by himself. It requires the womb (naturally and spiritually) of a woman. God had to open up Sarah's womb, but only after she endured her process. He could not produce a great nation through the womb of a barren and dominant woman who was destined for greatness. It was the good woman, Sarai who instructed her husband to lay with another woman to produce his seed. It was a good man who obeyed his wife. Wrong move! I hear so many men say, "A happy wife is a happy life." So not true in many cases.

Too many men are striving to make women, who are broken and dominant happy, which is only getting them in deeper situations such as distress, discontentment, and debt. A great woman understands that happiness is discovered internally. Any man or woman who looks externally for their solutions to life matters and/or circumstances are only setting themselves up for more destruction. As an example, God used Abraham and Sarah to execute His plan to restore our covenant agreement and relationship, so that His promises for our lives will be fulfilled.

In today's society, far too many great men have planted their sperm in the field (womb) of a broken woman, who birthed his son(s) and/or daughter(s). Unfortunately, children witness dominant women trying to break great men in the core of their soul. Many women may be upset to hear this truth, but dominant and controlling women who are harboring their pain (past or present) are victimizing their men. This is very prevalent amongst women in general, especially black women, due to our severe suffering during slavery.

Women of power, we must open our eyes to truth that a good man's inability to produce the promises of God for his life will keep your womb barren like Sarai. A barren womb can become a bitter soul if we don't understand a man's grief, as well as our own. As powerful as we are as women, we cannot physically heal a man's grief. Power doesn't heal. Money doesn't heal. Sex doesn't heal. Nothing but God's Spirit and original plan for our lives brings healing and restoration based upon His covenant agreement. The only thing a good man or woman has to do is totally surrender his or her will in obedience to Him, so he or she can begin the journey to greatness.

Out of Sarai's inability to give Abram a child, her heart and mind became as closed as her womb. In those days a woman who was unable to conceive a child for her husband was considered accursed. To be accursed, as the name implies is to live as if you are under a curse. Therefore, the effects of a curse can become prevalent in a woman's life, because of the pain and grief of the man in her life, which stems from her father. Remember, the man a woman attracts is always like unto her father. This is not a principle based on natural or physical appearances, but spiritual forces. This is unseen by the naked eye, but the damages manifest eventually.

For instance, look at many of our women in today's society, they have become dominant, abusive, and self-protective. Their hearts have become closed, especially to the pursuit of emotional healing and restoration. Like Sarai, many women disbelieve that God can do the impossible. Like Sarai, many women are carrying the grief of a good man and striving to fulfill his requests hoping to see change within their homes, communities, and churches. Just like God changed Abram's name to Abraham in order to validate him as a great man; he had to change Sarai's name to Sarah to do the same. God wants to change your name!

Too many women are trying to walk in their own shoes and identity to produce greatness, without waiting on God to change their name by way of the chosen great man for their lives. So many women believe that God has spoken to them, which He has and does all the time. However, my question is WHO is He speaking to, the good (dominant) woman or the great (submissive) woman? Before God changed Sarai's name, he first changed Abram's name to Abraham. God then spoke to Abraham about Sarai. He told him to no longer call her name Sarai, but Sarah. A great man can only identify his great woman according to God's instruction for his life.

When you hear the term grief, please don't limit it to death. Many men and women are grieving due to abandonment, rejection, and their lack of self-identity. Within my previous marriage, Initially, I received everything a woman could ever want or desire. It was filled with regard, love, adoration, and affirmation. Literally, he called me "Queen," and treated me as such. During these years with great stride he was becoming spiritually mature. However, he had not conquered places within his soul that were damaged from his past environment. This caused him to reach back to his former days. As I look back in hindsight, I realize that in order for God to spiritually perfect me, I had to experience the grief of my ex-husband in order to conquer my own, as he shared the same grief as my father.

The gates of hell came up against me. The purpose of these attacks was to rid my soul from filthiness (pride), naughtiness (control), lust (selfish desires) and superfluity (manipulation) that I inherited. The covenant of my father and mother, Abraham and Sarah, had to be restored in me. At this season of my life, I cannot be afraid to yield my will unto the great man God sends to me. It is imperative for me to come under his mission and vision. My womb must produce and birth the real awesome men (kings) promised to him as a spiritual father of many nations (Genesis 17:16). The love of Christ (agape) had to be engraved within my soul (mind and emotions) with meekness in order to do the will of Our Heavenly Father (James 1:21).

At this moment, I am reminded of a song by Jill Scott entitled "I Am Not Afraid"—search it online and listen to it. Sarah was not afraid to be everything she needed to be for the great man assigned to her life—Abraham. Whatever Abraham needed, Sarah possessed the beauty, grace, humility and fortitude for him to make provisions. The changing of her name from Sarai (dominant princess) to Sarah (submissive queen) was the change she experienced in her heart to birth kings placed in her womb by the great man – Abraham. Well, great man and great woman, so it is in the natural realm so it is divinely ordained spiritually. Your position in life is for your posterity.

Great Man Where Art Thou? Our nations are waiting…

GREAT MAN WHERE ART THOU?

The Silent Cry of a Woman's Heart...

AGE: 37
STATUS: SINGLE
RESIDE: CHICAGO, IL

Overall, I believe great men still exist. It's like trying to find a needle in a haystack, because so many are not acting in greatness. I also believe many great men aren't seen because a lot of them want to remain humble and behind the scenes. They don't want to draw a lot of attention to themselves in order to keep integrity and godly character intact. In addition, I believe majority of great men in the African American community are in prison for whatever reason, but they have greatness within them. It's just the way that the system works. There are many who are not, but I believe they are stifled or hidden behind what is going on in the world. What I mean is, technology and different vices pull men from spiritual leadership roles where they have moral values, dignity and integrity. Many men are negating moral values, the importance of family, and faithful marriages to one wife. I believe that the devil uses different tactics that appeal to great men. Even in greatness they fall victim making poor decisions.

One life lesson that I would share with women is in reference to a bible scripture: that a man who finds a wife finds a good thing (Proverbs 18:22). I want to use that as a catalyst that a woman should not search for a man or husband. Also, they should not manipulate the situation and play God in order to get that man to like her, or be in a relationship with her. Although it might seem good, it's not. He may not be what God wanted for her, and the broader picture. Women, don't put yourself in a situation with a good man: he could be a friend, a co-worker, or somebody you know at church. Don't try to pull him to you. If he's interested he's going to pursue you. If he's a Godly man he should know the word. He will court you, which may or may not progress to love.

I'm not discouraging friendly flirting or at least letting a man know you are interested, but what I am merely saying, "Do not play God." You may like this guy, and know what turns him on; however, to lure him, manipulating the situation, and lying about who you really are, can turn out to be very explosive. I'm specifically saying to women, "Just be yourself in all cases." Be real, but more importantly be very patient and allow the man to pursue you.

I take my role as a father seriously because it's a moral responsibility. I made the decision to have a child. Therefore, it's my obligation to be responsible for her. Parenthood is not always planned, and as parents, we don't always agree, but no matter what happens we have an obligation to take care of our children. In fact, they never asked to be born. They are young, vulnerable and need parental guidance. They need their mother, father, grandmother, grandfather, aunts and uncles. They need the community to help raise them to provide those moral values, education, life examples and experiences. What they need most is love when they are of a younger age, but also as they grow. For me, it is a true gift from God to have a child. The bible tells us to multiply and subdue the earth. With that regard, we're to take opportunities to increase our family, and have dominion in this world. In order to keep a legacy going, it's good to have children whether you adopt, foster a child, or give birth. However they come, it's our responsibility to help raise them. As they grow up, we should encourage them to pave the way, and create a family plan that will help us as seniors. I want to be able to leave a legacy for my daughter and then allow her to leave legacies for her children and future generations. In the meantime, I will share the gospel with her and teach her to pray at a young age. Also, I will teach her to have morals and values. I hope that she will keep those teachings and eventually share them. When she becomes married and have children, I hope she does the same.

Unfortunately, when I experienced my first broken heart, it was with my mom. She was a single parent with five sons. She often chased after men, based on issues she had in her own life growing up. Initially, my mom wasn't really there in my life, so I didn't have the training. I didn't have a father figure that stayed in my life. Also, I was in the house alone a lot while growing up. I also took care of my little brothers. I wasn't sure how to handle that initial heart break, so I went into survival mode for over thirty years. It wasn't until a few years ago that I started meeting with a counselor about this situation. I began learning that expressing emotion was good. When you have heartbreak, it is okay to be sad about it; so I now allow those emotions to come out. I find myself being emotional even sometimes just watching movies if they have a certain theme or affect. The way I now deal with heartbreak is by allowing a period of time for reflection, to see what I've done to contribute; and then what I could do better in the next instance. That's actually how I'm dealing with being a single man and also a single father. I'm looking back and reviewing all the things that I've done, the poor choices and the decisions I've made; and allowing myself to be healed. Then I will move forward, starting from scratch with 100 percent trust, not bringing any old baggage with me. I am able to forgive those who have caused me pain, in order to be free from bondage; so I can live and love as a godly man.

Chapter Four

AGREE TO DISAGREE

In Amos 3:3 the question is asked, "Can two walk together, except they be agreed?" In the spirit of that question is the knowledge that good and great will never see eye to eye. Good possesses one view about life, while great possesses another. Good is based upon ordinary, while great is based upon extraordinary. Good thinks it can stand alone, great knows it needs others like itself to produce greatness.

It is unfortunate that in the times which we live, too many **great** men are submitting to the vision of a **good** woman. Submission has to be symbiotic for ultimate success to be achieved. Great men are living beneath their God-given authority, dominion and rule. They are compromising to keep peace with others, and losing sight of intentional living. For example, if a man gives a woman her way all the time, it may seem right to her, but it may not be right for him. He has the potential to lose a part of himself in the process, which can become a problem.

There is no absolute right or wrong between man and woman; the only thing that keeps them united as one is TRUTH. They each have their own views, which must be unified based upon one common denominator, The Manufacturer, who created both. This will be discussed in a later chapter, but in summary: Man and Woman were created to work in a unified manner towards a God-given purpose, mission and vision. We must understand this from a collective perspective, as opposed to an individual one. On far too many occasions, we are attempting to view "Life" from the same perspective when God has given each of us (man and woman) our own insight. This is how we miss opportunities that can work in our favor as a united front. We must work the mission together with no division. That's the power of agreement! By contrast, a good man or woman may strive to be faithful to the cause and end up failing, because his or her focus becomes distracted. Temporary gratifications for immediate gain can be used to create division and disagreement.

Good men and good women can be overly concerned about having a relationship. They don't think to evaluate upfront whether they even share the same core beliefs. They enter into their relationship carrying two visions, which is di-vision. This is because of their difference in views and opinions. Division is the deceptive root of any relationship that leads to destruction. This breeds confusion and discord. Energy is wasted because one is always trying to get the other to submit.

According to I Corinthians 14:33, God is not the author of confusion. Let me blow your mind: Satan isn't either! Confusion starts when the man and woman have not positioned or aligned themselves to the order and rank established by God. This misalignment breeds pride and stubbornness, which leads to strife and contention (Proverbs 28:25). The safest place is in the perfect (mature) plan of God. The life of a man and woman is destined for chaos when they are not in total submission to God, as well as each other. Real submission is a three-fold cord that is not easily broken (Ecclesiastes 4:12).

Great men and women walk in the power of agreement, because they share the same core beliefs and press towards the prize of their higher calling daily. Because of this, cohesiveness between a great man and woman is less challenging. They are focused on establishing a solid relationship and friendship, which develops peace amongst them. The power of agreement stems from mindsets that are congruent with God's will for their lives. Just because two people are together does not mean they are in agreement. A **great** man coupled with a **good** woman will never produce this.

The relationship will eventually lose its burning fire with them always striving to rekindle the flame of romance. When a **great** man and a **great** woman are joined together, each can remain authentic with their visions and views. They discover ways to always remain unified based upon their purpose. This eliminates discord and strife. They push one another to greater heights, because iron sharpens iron (Proverbs 27:17). When a great man finds a great woman, she is working on the vision given to her by God. They each recognize that it's their time to live out all that has been invested.

A great man communicates with a great woman intentionally to explore the depths of her mind and to learn of her character. He places demands without being demanding, because his purpose places great demands on him. For a woman with unhealed wounds, these demands will expose the weakness of her character. The damaged mindset of a good woman will make her fearful and insecure. She may take offense to her weaknesses being exposed. Her infirmities will give place to the devil within her soul, as a deadly trap to be used against the man while fulfilling his vision.

On the other hand, the mindset of a woman endeavoring to be great will see her weaknesses as an opportunity to be strengthened with God's help. She does not fear being vulnerable. When you remain focused on vision at all cost, love covers and conquers all your deficits! We must operate in this agape love consistently and intentionally. It is the closest person to a great man or woman that can serve as a stumbling block. Beware! This stems from past unhealed wounds in the soul (mind and emotions). Women, we must become emotionally healed to walk in our greatness.

During the course of me writing this chapter, I had the privilege of hearing the heart of a great man, who is seeking for a great woman committed to God. The five attributes and qualities he expressed ignites the power of agreement, so a great man and woman can walk together harmoniously. They are as follows:

UNDERSTANDING

To a great man, understanding is a valuable commodity and very hard to find. A great woman has her own sphere of influence. Often these two domains collide and make the journey difficult at times. Having an understanding, merges the two entities, as they remain relentless about their vision. It works out all the bumps in the road (Proverbs 4:7).

DRIVE

A great man is drawn to a woman who has a drive towards mission and vision. However, her motivation behind the drive must include his interest as well, which brings common ground. Their mutuality makes the relationship long lasting and fulfilling. Drive is the substance that helps build their friendship and relationship.

INFLUENCE

A great man is drawn to a woman of influence. She uses this characteristic to lead others, restore people in their faith, and bring unity. Her influence is exemplified out of genuine love and regard for people. This helps him move his mission, and promote his ability to carry out his vision as a leader. She supports him while winning the hearts and earning the trust of others.

SENSITIVITY

A great man admires a woman who is sensitive without wearing her feelings on her sleeve. She is tender in her dealings with him, yet firm in her stance. She is sensitive enough to speak the truth in love without bruising him. This keep his heart fortified to persevere in times of difficulties and stay focused on the cause. In her lies a place of refuge from the battlefield, as she encourages him to fight and overcome.

WARMTH

A great man appreciates the safety and security provided by a woman's warmth. She is filled with dignity and discretion. Her tender heart allows him to be vulnerable. It is her grace and gratitude for the simple things in life that keeps him pressing to bring her the finest things in life. Not only is she a graceful woman, but a grateful woman. He appreciates the protection and peace that her warmth provides for him.

Do these qualities resonate with you? When I heard this great man share what he needed from a great woman, it made me realize that I had been displaying these qualities to good men. It was because of their past pains that made me walk out of agreement with my true self at one point in time. Emotional healing restored my self-worth. Now, I display these attributes with caution, as I fulfill my God-given mission and vision.

As a great woman, I am sure that you have exhibited these attributes as well, probably without realizing it. As a result, all of us have been hurt and disappointed. I cannot express the necessity of emotional healing. Whether that great man is a father, husband, brother, son, or friend, please be assured that they need you to be your true self. This requires healing and humility. It is not always easy, but it is necessary.

GREAT MAN WHERE ART THOU?

The Silent Cry of a Woman's Heart...

AGE: 27
STATUS: SINGLE
RESIDE: MADISON, WISCONSIN

Today, I believe that great men are in the places where they are needed whether in the community, doing active organizing or activism. They're in education (i.e. schools), and basically in various places as needed. I know there's a lot of turmoil. The perception of what men are supposed to be, especially black men, has been distorted throughout generations. I feel like there are a few great men still out there taking their rightful place in their families, communities, and churches. They are positioned where they should be or where they can be best utilized. I think great men are both married and single. Similar to me, the single men are by themselves for a reason. It isn't time for them to be married.

The one thing that drives me crazy about women now days, specifically younger women, is that they should really value themselves and know their self-worth. This is one lesson that any woman, young or older, can learn because social media has taken over. It seems like a lot of these women today are crying out for attention. With social media, followers equal attention, fame, etc. As a result, their self-worth is being distorted or defined by social media views. I think really knowing their value and true identity can be the biggest lessons to learn, and knowing how they should be defined.

I feel like a woman can only give another woman a certain perspective regarding her true identity. However, a woman getting this information from a female, who has not yet developed into a woman, who understands her worth, will not provide her with the proper guidance of who she needs to be. Honestly, she can acquire a lot of information just by reading the bible, along with other supporting literature. How she was raised plays a part as well. It is equally important that a woman learns about her true identity from a guy's perspective. Lastly, seeking a mentor to direct and shape her to be the woman she should be is an added value to her development.

When I become a father, I will take care of my children because I was responsible for them being in this world. It is my obligation to share my duty as a father, raise them and lead my household. It is very prevalent in research and in life, that fatherless kids fare worse than kids who come from homes where fathers are present. This can have long term detrimental effects not only academically but emotionally and socially.

I only experienced a broken heart one time and we were both fairly young. Basically, I just had to let her get out what it was she had to say in the situation and be there to listen. At that point, her heart was already broken and there was no turning back. There was nothing I could really say or do to change it. I just let her get out frustrations and everything she had to say from what happened in that situation. What happened between us was an informative situation.

Moving forward, when I encounter the next woman, I will do things differently. It sucks that somebody had to be a sacrifice in a sense for me to learn a lesson. Today, I try to avoid having a broken heart and to prevent certain things from getting to that point. It is avoidable in a sense. My previous situation could've been avoided if I knew what I know now, but sometimes things just don't work. When you break up with somebody their heart might be broken really bad. What can you do about that?

Now, I am open and honest and have a conversation when I don't think she is the one that I need to be with. As men, we need to be upfront and let them know, so we avoid that kind of broken heart scenario. Once you have that upfront conversation it is going to save you a lot of time, energy, and wasted effort in the long run. Women have to be receptive to somebody being honest with them. Honestly, I feel like the worst thing a woman could ever hear is a guy saying, "I don't want to be with you."

I feel like today's women and men, no matter who they are, seem so thirsty to be with or even to talk to someone. For example, when a guy says, "I am cool that's not what I'm on, you're a nice person, but no thank you," women don't know how to take that. Then all of sudden the guy is either gay or he's this or he's that. In all actuality, a woman needs to really listen to what he's saying, and be glad that he told her without getting into a relationship, and even sleep with her. Being honest keeps her from looking stupid six months or a year down the line, because she did not listen in the beginning when he told her she's not what he wanted. She could have been receptive and moved on like an adult. Personally, I have seen this happen so many times, especially, if she is really attractive. Nowadays, women don't take "No" very well, especially girls who are used to guys falling all over them.

Chapter Five

FEAR FACTOR

I don't believe the fear that a great man possesses is a fear of commitment to a great woman; but actually a fear of commitment to God. A true commitment to God requires him to surrender his own mind, view and way of thinking. Many great men have become so self-sufficient that they magnify themselves as opposed to God. The great man must yield and humble himself, so that he can submit to his God ordained mission and vision; which requires him to surrender his total will.

One of our most influential examples of a great man is Abram. God established a covenant with him, which required one of the most radical changes in his life. Abram had to separate from his kin and country in order to walk in his true identity. What a sacrifice! The very first thing God spoke to him was "Fear not, I am thy shield, and thy exceeding great reward." -Genesis 15:1 KJV. **"Fear not"** literally means **"revere not".** God was aware that He was speaking to a man who was living by the mindset that was instilled in him through his environment and upbringing. He was raised in a place called Haran, which was a land filled with grief. As a result of his pain and dysfunction, Abram revered himself and his abilities, not God. In order for Abram to receive what God had for him, he first had to move away from his kinfolk, traditions, and religiosity, so he could clearly hear from God and believe in himself as the great man.

Many great men today are in a similar state due to their past. They are great men who are stuck with disbelief and grief. Too often they are looking to themselves for the answers, only to discover they alone are not the solution. The great man must humble himself. He must communicate with God and obey His voice. When he does, he will walk in the covenant that has been ordained for his life; and God will get the glory.

God will use certain circumstances and situations that will cause the great man to look to Him. Strategically, He moves the great man out of his own way. God wants to endow him with a vast commission, but His first commandment is that he **"revere not"** himself. In revering God, he will not only receive a great reward, but the Lord thy God will do exceedingly and abundantly above all he could ever, ask, think or imagine. (Ephesians 3:20).

The great woman must also be in a posture where she does not fear (revere herself), understanding that her reward is not in man, but in God. She must continue to stand and not give up on what she sees and believes. Her faith is enough! Her sons and daughters will reap the promises spoken based upon the covenant given to Abraham, which was to restore man and woman in their rightful place of dominion. The great woman always stands in truth, worship and authenticity of whose she is, recognizing who she was created to be for her family and legacy.

However, the strategy is different for the great woman who encounters that great man who still holds "fears" due to past disappointments, traumas and/or betrayals. This hinders him from committing to God and woman. As she becomes emotionally invested with the great man, his fears can become her fears. Beware! Because she has personally endured processes of change causing her to yield to God's will for her life, it won't stop her. Yet, she can be hindered if not aware of his past encounters that caused him grief and pain, especially in relationships with other women. It is God's responsibility to provoke the thoughts of that man by awakening his soul and spirit. This type of relationship with God will cause emotional healing and restoration. The promises for his life and legacy shall be released based upon the covenant made to our forefathers; Abraham, Isaac & Jacob.

I am reminded of Proverbs 31 where we find specifics qualities to what type of woman the great man requires. She must know how to utilize her mind and hands, take care of her household and truly serve a great man based upon his mission. This lifestyle is not only for her benefit, but also for the great man in her life and their family.

In Proverbs 31:1, King Lemuel's mother, a great woman, taught him the characteristics of this type of woman, as well as prophesied to him concerning his future and destiny. She instructed him not to consume strong drink, or give his strength to women. King Lemuel's mother admonished that he preserve himself, without fear, and live a lifestyle of reverence and worship unto God. As his mother, she spoke life into him and esteemed him from the womb.

Most great men in this era of time are lacking mothers such as King Lemuel's; who spoke precisely to her son based upon his greatness. Many great men are still in need of women of this caliber. It is evident that our men (who are sons first) still require great women, who preserves their heart for greatness, to speak into their lives.

In Ephesians 6:12, Apostle Paul lets us know that our warfare is not with flesh and blood (people), but against principalities (spiritual forces). This is not a focal point, because our eyes are trained to see people. However, we typically comprehend this passage as a general statement, but it is very specific in nature. I believe that this spiritual principle is speaking primarily to the mother (great woman) who has been positioned in a household, so that the legacy planted in her womb and birthed is intentionally lived out.

It takes a great woman to spiritually fight and cry out to God on behalf of the great men, so they will conquer their fears. She must endure! It can become difficult at times because her emotional needs are not always being met. Her worship will cause her to become grounded and face her own struggles. She must remain in the presence of God so that He will bring continuously healing to her heart. The main thing to understand, as a great woman, is that you are always conquering the spirit of fear on behalf of great men in your life.

I want to bring comfort to every woman's heart who is continuously fighting and believing for deliverance of the great men in her life. It is not God's will that any man should perish. However, we all have decisions to make that must line up with His will for our lives. Continue to pray and worship! As we grow, develop and complete assignments according to God's directives; we are abolishing our own fears through obedience. This does not always feel good, but be encouraged that He will never leave or forsake you. Only God can contend with man; we as women cannot. God will commune with His men who were made in His image and likeness according to their mission and commission. Man belongs to God, and woman was divinely given to mankind for intentional living, and to be loved. If the men in your life seem not to cherish you as the great woman you are, God will strategically establish the required course of action according to His predestined plans.

In conclusion, I want to affirm you: know that you are a great woman and a part of that plan! Every strategy consists of a long term goal which requires implementing certain dynamics, so let patience mature on the inside of you. I want to share strategies with you that I use when fear tries to infiltrate my heart and soul. I had to learn how to turn my fear into faith by taking what was designed to work against me, and use it to work for me. This is a constant process. The only thing that empowers me to carry out these strategies is my true love for the Word of God. I strive to live by spiritual principles and apply them to my everyday life. I encourage you as a great woman to do the same. Using them on a daily basis guarantees successful outcomes.

Based upon my own experiences, I have taken the term *FEAR* and made it an acronym to shift my paradigm when things appear to be impossible. Working this strategy has been proven in my life. It's not always easy, but I must say, "It works!" Nonetheless, it has produced peace in my life and relationships on every hand. I hope you implement them in the relationships you have with the great men in your life.

F = FRIENDSHIP

Proverbs 18:24 *A man (woman) that hath friends must shew himself friendly; and there is a friend that sticketh closer than a brother.*

Every great man lays a foundation of friendship with a great woman. As women, we desire to be in relationship with them before a firm friendship has been established. This consists of trust, honesty, candor, and respect. He needs to be assured that you got his back, especially when life challenges arise. A great man likes the "real deal". Take a minute to journal how you can become a better friend to the great men in your life or the one you aspire to have.

_____

_____

_____

_____

_____

_____

_____

_____

_____

_____

_____

_____

_____

_____

E – ESTEEM

Romans 1:18 NKJV *For the wrath of God is revealed from heaven against all ungodliness and unrighteousness of men, who suppress the truth in unrighteousness.*

Men were created in the likeness and image of God with truth wrought on the inside of them. Therefore, building them up is key for them to gain a greater understanding of their true identity. This produces wholesome outcomes for continued success. A man should never to be torn down physically or verbally. We see the damaging effects of this in our communities. Esteeming them causes the truth that has been residing deep within them to come alive, permeating their hearts and minds. Women, the words we use in our conversations, as well as our mannerism are vital. A great man thrives on words filled with quality not quantity. His identity requires esteem, especially when his actions do not warrant it. Implementing this strategy will show you how powerful you really are as a great woman. Take another minute to assess the words you use. What a difference one word can make! Write sentences and quality phrases that can be used to build them up based upon God's word:

_____

_____

_____

_____

_____

_____

_____

_____

A = ADORATION

Genesis 12:3 *I will bless those who bless you, And I will curse those who curses you; And in you all the families in the earth shall be blessed.*

In the beginning of this chapter, I mentioned that Abram was a great man. Through his obedience, he became a descendant of God, to receive the blessing promised to him. Women we are not exempt. Too many of us perceive the term **"bless"** to be of monetary value. We must understand that **bless** means *to kneel as an act of adoration*. Am I referring this in a literal sense? Not really. But I am admonishing you to humble yourself as a figurative means of adoration. Remember, the promise of God is for you to be blessed as well. As a great woman, God adores you when you can humble yourself unto Him first and foremost. Regardless of the actions of a man, God will honor your actions as you implement His strategies. I am a living witness that this will cause a great man to grow not only closer to you, but more importantly to God. Just stay in a posture of adoration and worship unto Him without complaining and murmuring. When it gets difficult to adore someone who does not adore you back, go into worship and ADORE the One who will never leave or forsake you. Please take a few minutes to journal your adoration unto Our Father. In the same way you communicate to Him, use those same words to esteem and affirm a great man.

_____

_____

_____

_____

R = RESPECT

Ephesians 5:33 *Nevertheless let everyone of you in particular so love his wife even as himself; and the wife see that she respects (reverence) her husband.*

During the course of my previous marriage, I learned how to apply this strategic plan almost to perfection. It truly took the love of God working through me. I had to die to self on many occasions by bridling my tongue. What a task! The key to this is to not say anything if you have nothing good to say. We must keep our hearts and minds pure and wholesome through prayer and meditation, so when we speak our words and behaviors will be respectful. Please don't hinder your blessing by limiting this to husbands. Before a man becomes a husband he is a man and will always be. As women, we were not admonished to love men more than to respect them. Our respect for them exudes from our love, which work hand in hand with friendship, esteem and adoration. Please take a few minutes to journal how you can give respect even the more to the great men in your life.

_____

_____

_____

_____

_____

_____

_____

_____

_____

GREAT MAN WHERE ART THOU?
The Silent Cry of a Woman's Heart...

AGE: 33
STATUS: MARRIED
RESIDE: BIRMINGHAM, ALABAMA

There are still a lot of great men; I just feel that many of them have been misguided. Media, as well as social media; does a great job of painting a picture that good and great men are virtually non-existent, especially black men. There are many men who are educated and well-groomed; everyone is not a rapper or drug-dealer type. My personal opinion is that a lot of women may be searching for the caliber of a great man in the wrong places. Not only is the view of some women off, but there are many who have an expectation of perfection in men. The honest truth is that there is so much that men have to LEARN about how to be great men; in order to be the spiritual men, husbands, fathers, and financial leaders that women need. Those are big shoes to fill, and a lot of roles to achieve. I encourage our women to support and stand by their men, especially in tough times. You may feel like we should already know how to do these things; but please just remain patient and supportive in every way, especially sexually, as we go through our growing process. As you stand by your man, in the long run it will pay off.

One thing that helped me was I had a great example. Even though my parents were divorced while I was growing up, my dad was still in the picture; and my mom fully endorsed that. She never prevented me from seeing my dad, and always allowed me to cherish the relationship I had with him with no negative interference. One of the most important things my dad taught me was to always take care of my mom and my sister. I owned that when I got my own family, and I continue to do the same for them by any means necessary. It is my duty, position and God-given right to take care of my family; and I'm not defaulting that honor to another man.

I know God put the right person in my life to help me through trying times, my wife. She supports me in challenging times, even when I'm not doing exactly what she wants. There are moments that she kind of put me in my place, but she does it with wisdom and understanding. Sometimes she's like "Hey, I know you don't know everything, neither do I; but what I do know is that this not the right direction to go." She is not confrontational, but she is direct. I really thank her for that. I am grateful for my wife and also my two daughters. They teach me how to love.

As a man, I haven't always done well in this area. I was not good in handling a broken heart; and I acted out towards women. Sometimes it's really difficult for men to tap into the emotional side of themselves, but when they do they tend to love hard. This makes anything that goes wrong much more difficult to get over. I became that stereotypical man (playboy and dog) as a result of my hurt. I was scared of getting my heart broken again, and did everything in my power to prevent it from happening. Ultimately, the only thing that helped me was getting closer to God and learning about Him.

Men handle a broken heart or betrayal in different ways. Prior to changing my life, seeking God's wisdom and then becoming a husband, I handled my wounds by cheating on women. It became very hard to be faithful, because my guard was definitely up. So many men just don't know how to deal with struggles and pain in relationships. Some may even turn to physical violence. I thank God for the help He sent me, and even before my wife and girls; I had my sister and mother. They kept me grounded. I think about the holidays in my younger years while still in college. Guys would take that special girl home with them, and at one point I was bringing a different girl home for every occasion. My mom and sister noticed the pattern, so they sat down and had a conversation with me. It made me stop and smell the coffee. I realized this is not the direction I needed to head in; it was leading to destruction for me and the women.

Now that I have my two daughters, I think about what it will be like for them when they begin to date, and I strive to set a strong example for them. I want them to connect with men who have similar attributes that remind them of their father in a positive, Godly, and healthy way. I want them to have husbands who treat them the way they aspire to be treated. I want them to witness that based upon how I treated their mother. I'm living this right path not only for myself, but also for my family.

Chapter Six

I AM BEAUTIFUL

In Proverbs 13:22 it says a good man (great man) leaves an inheritance for his children and his children's children. Legacy continues as that man marries, and she becomes the mother of his children. That man will attract a woman based upon the attributes he witnessed in his mother. The reason our generations is growing worse and worse is because of the absence of God's order in the family dynamic. Not only is the presence of great men in many homes missing, but also the absence of the great woman's beauty, because of her overwhelming obligations.

When a great woman's beauty is diminished, she becomes a good woman who ends up 'doing' tasks and duties all the time. Sadly, a good man will LET her, even though she is so depleted. He'll sit there like he's the king of the castle, because he feels good about being served by her. Because he works a job, he thinks he can just sit on the couch while she does the laundry, the cooking, the kids, and everything else. He sees her "do, do, do," without providing a foundation for her inner beauty to shine on his behalf. She is so tired when she goes to bed, but yet a good man wants her to 'do' sex amongst all other duties. It's not making love any more, it's just sex.

As long as he releases, he is satisfied. She just opened her legs to do it! Many of them [good men] get their satisfaction, turn over and go to sleep while the woman is left without a climax. Her beauty is diminished, as she feels demoralized on the inside. Been their done that, and I'm sure that I am not alone. Too many women feel this way, which is the silent cry of their heart. But, I am a living witness that God will deliver and set you free. That's why it is imperative that we, great women, must come into agreement with our true beauty to take our power back to **be** the great women we were created to **be**!

When a great man and woman come together sexually it is **be**cause of their worship and warfare. They sleep and stand together based on their God given mission and vision, and what God has revealed to her. Sex was created for intentional living filled with pleasure. Therefore, when SHE climaxes on her man, it's not strictly about the sexual feeling. It's about releasing the silent cry of her heart in worship. It is not just to wet his penis, but to cover his heart. Their unified minds, stemming from an unselfish and sacrificial love; empowers them to experience sexual intercourse that is truly mind-blowing. This realm of living was originally constructed by Our Creator for man and woman to have true intimacy with one another. This experience is based upon who they are as a united force, and both experiencing a climax strengthens them to take on more due to their life's mission. His release into her allows him to deposit the cares of this world that attempted to weigh on his heart, mind and soul to hinder his progress. This is his warfare.

Apostle Paul admonishes every man in 1 Corinthians 7:2 to have his own wife; and every woman to have her own husband. When a man cannot take the time to bring his woman to an orgasm, he is not taking advantage of the opportunity to experience her worship. This fortifies and strengthens her fight and warfare on behalf of her family and legacy. A great man was made to see the fruit of his labor. A great man cannot carry the weight of the world without releasing his cares into his great woman whom he trusts. Intercourse is his primary method of communication that expresses his innermost self, which coincides and ignites his verbal. A great man doesn't trust just any woman with his heart. A great woman is the one (womb bearer) chosen, created and equipped to bear his mind (sperm) ejaculated into her soul; heart, mind and body. That's what reproduction is all about, and that is how legacy lives. This is a beautiful thing! When sex is scattered abroad, life becomes perverted, homes become broken and children are left hurting. As a result, legacies are destroyed.

Keep in mind that a great woman was taken out of a great man, so the ability to handle multiple responsibilities was innately placed in the core of her being. Due to the man's substance that she received, she executes skillfully and effectively. This is what makes her so beautiful. True beauty is beyond her outward appearance. However, this is never to be dismissed. This is what makes her great!

The great woman will carry on with tasks and services that God requires of her. She keeps moving based on what God endowed deep within her soul and spirit. It extends beyond her home and immediate surroundings, as well as her children, family and friends. The great woman thinks from a perspective that allows her to reach the masses. Her focus to live an intentional life leaves little room for devoting her thoughts to the whereabouts of a man, whether he is deemed good or great. Because she is obedient to what God has assigned to her hands, He is always attentive to the silent cry of her heart.

The energy a great woman exerts daily keeps her moans and groans deep within as a sweet fragrance unto God. Her greatest desire is that the great men in her life and surroundings be in covenant relationship with Christ; so that they are always experiencing healing, restoration and rejuvenation. This kind of beauty gives her a *"Peace"* that most don't understand. Yet, she smiles and laughs all while her heart may be bleeding on the inside. Her inner beauty keeps her fortified so the dormant places within the men in her life will be resurrected, as their eyes are open to truth. No matter what, spiritually, she sees the great men in her life walking with God.

I am reminded of so many women who I've witnessed exemplifying their beauty in the midst of struggles. My mother was one of those great women. Women of old endured so many trials and tribulations, but maintained their grace to serve mankind with kindness, gentleness, and humility. In addition, they believed in standing with their men in spite of what they knew or saw them do. Wow! That's a beauty beyond compare. These women were deemed beautiful, because of their ability to handle circumstances without belittling themselves or controlling their men. I believe that a great woman always walks in her beauty no matter what is transpiring with great men due to their indiscretions or challenges. Integrity motivates her relentless stance to do what's right at all times with a pure heart.

A great woman understands just how valuable and pliable a man's heart is even with its broken places. Every word that she speaks out of her mouth will be spoken to build him up. If she doesn't have anything good to say, then she does not speak at all. We have lost this skill and art of knowing when to speak and when to be silent. However, we must get it back. It's crucial that we maintain our composure in order to regain this kind of beauty that reflects our lineage, and the character of women who have gone on before us. Great men need great women in their midst who know how to stand with confidence and assurance. Often times, the power of a silent woman can go further than her words which make her beautiful beyond compare. Words are seeds, and seeds germinate. Remember, God reveals to a great woman! The woman will receive revelations as her beauty is constantly tested and proven to be able to handle the truth. As a result, the great man is able to be nourished by her beauty, which will cause his internal fears and struggles to be demolished.

A great man or woman cannot **be** totally effective in their responsibilities without a **cause**. It leads them to being o**be**dient to God's will. Because they were made to be great and powerful (which is one in the same) they impact lives whether they realize it or not. For every cause there is an effect. It is imperative that every woman gains a deeper understanding of her greatness and the power she possesses. Having this understanding keeps her focused so she doesn't veer from their cause, mission and vision. At times, this can become difficult to keep sight of, and operate in because her duties can become routine, mundane and thankless.

The great man and woman both have roles designated within their partnership. Some are specifically assigned, others are interchangeable. Some are communicated and conveyed, and others are innately adapted to. The main point that needs to be emphasized here is that these areas are directly tied into who God created each of them to be in the earth, while utilizing their gifts and talents for their vision and mission. Both are mature enough to understand that they were created, molded and shaped by God for the benefit of one another and the relationship. This is a beautiful thing!

Although men and women were designed to work together, historically, women were created to undergird one another as they helped their men fulfill their purpose. One of the biggest hindrances today to men operating in their sure purpose is the fact that women don't stand together, naturally or spiritually. When a woman is giving birth to a baby, she is never alone. In times of old, the mother and the midwives were most important to the birth of the child than the doctor. It was the women who were wiping her forehead, holding her hand, speaking encouragement and comfort, and preparing water. Men did not enter the birthing room when she was in labor. They stayed on the outside waiting on the announcement of whether they were the father of a son or daughter. The word would excitedly come from one of the women who had gone through the process with the mother, and was genuinely happy for her.

Even after birth, children became as much as the midwives' responsibility for future success as the mother. Not just to give them gifts or spoil them, but to give them instructions and guidance. What the mother was not able to see, it was picked up by the auntie, the sister, the friend, the grandmother, or the elder...all women who had the mother's back. Women counted on each other in the home, community, church, school and vineyard so that the children remained on course.

Great women, we have lost this level of sisterhood, the commodity of travailing and birthing together (naturally and spiritually) on behalf of our great men. So much has become distorted in the minds and hearts of women in today's society, which is hindering our men; sons, brothers, uncles, nephews, etc. Our desire to witness each other blessed and adored has been clouded by dissension, complications, jealousy, strife, envy, isolations, bickering, bitterness, gossiping, backbiting and betrayal. Unfortunately, sleeping with other women's' husbands and crossing various boundaries has become a norm. We, as great women must realize that a man can't cause us to betray one another unless we permit him.

Our beauty requires us to remain faithful to ourselves, as our sisters (great women) become our benefactors. It is time for our eyes to be open to truth that the enemy is succeeding in keeping women divided, so his plans prevail. This is having a direct hit on our men, as we are leaving our battle post to get in the ring with one another.

From a natural standpoint, wars are mainly fought by men. However, from a spiritual standpoint; there is a major part of the fight that is given to women by God. The warfare of a great man is to hear and obey. The worship of a great woman is to be who God created her to be no matter what. The enemy of every man (king) can't stand to behold the beauty of a great woman (queen) in her position. Like the game of chess, a queen (great woman) can move anywhere she likes in protection of her king (great man). That's why we must be in position to fight in obedience to our cause; family and legacy. A great woman (queen) stands united with other women, praying for strength in her inner man.

God is watching us, and we must be mindful that He is omniscient and omnipresent. It's not what we do in public that gets the reward, but how we live reflecting the private domains of our heart. Our Heavenly Father is looking at His daughters, who have been given wombs to birth His plans for our family and legacy. As great women, I believe that as we cleanse and purify our hearts before God, we will see astounding changes in our homes, communities, workplaces, society, country and nations.

Women, there are so many responsibilities expected of us that wants to keep us fulfilling duties without embracing our true beauty. Please don't fall prey to this snare and trap for your life. I am a living witness that it will rob you of your freedom to BE the great woman that you were created to BE. So, I encourage you to rise up within your strength and power, and proclaim with boldness **"I Am Beautiful!"** Continue working God's plan and purpose for your life and declare that the great men in your life shall be healed and set free from all that is hindering them from walking in their greatness. In this proclamation and declaration you will continuously discover more of you – the beautiful woman you are.

GREAT MAN WHERE ART THOU?

The Silent Cry of a Woman's Heart...

AGE: 44
STATUS: DIVORCED
RESIDE: CHICAGO, ILLINOIS

There aren't too many great men around today like when I was growing up; a lot of them have been destroyed by drugs and the criminal system. However, back in the day there were a lot of them who I looked up to. Some who had a profound influence on me became involved with the dark side. I'm not sure what contributed to such a great demise, but I believe part of it was poor judgment. Some of these men were naïve to their associations. I have friends who went down that path, but I'm glad to say that many of them have made changes in their lives for the better. One of my friends, who is a mechanic was recently working on my vehicle. He was reminiscing about his younger years, all the nice things he had before his downfall, especially the cars. When I asked him how it all changed, he told me how hanging out with the wrong people brought enticement to do drugs, and he gave in.

I work in the medical field, and I serve a lot of IV drug users. Sometimes conversations come up that tell their stories of how they started using. It always blows my mind, because when I was growing up there was just a strong knowing in me to say "No!" I remember watching a PSA announcement that came on TV. It showed the effects of drugs on a person's life; including death in some cases. I took that to heart, because I didn't want to die. I saw real life examples pertaining to drugs that ruined many people's lives. They lost good jobs, and went on downward spirals in every area of living. I knew I didn't want to go down that road.

When there is a lack of great men, it becomes very hard to raise young men to become great. We have to be the examples. There are certain things a woman can teach a boy, but there are other things he can only learn from his father or a man who is a father figure. It is very disappointing and many young males are suffering as a result. It is also very tough on the women raising sons.

As a man, I have stepped in with women in these situations. For friends, there have been times that I spend with their boys (and girls as well) doing enriching activities. We have to be involved, not just to raise them with TV and video games, but interaction. There are other programs that I suggest as well, avenues that may provide mentorship to the children; community centers and churches being on the top of the list. Children need positive reinforcement. This benefits the entire household. I help find resources when I am not able to give of my time, personally. I also encourage the mothers to pay attention to the child such as; who their friends are, and what environments they're entering into. This is critical, because everyone can't be trusted. But above all, I encourage women not to give up, even when life and parenting get difficult.

I know this because I'm a father myself. I took the responsibility very serious when they were children, and I am still very much a part of their adult lives. I was blessed to have my father when I was growing up as well. He wasn't just in my life, but he lived with me, raised me and was married to my mother. I recall a time when I was in the third grade, my dad asked me a question that challenged my perspective of something I hadn't given thought to before then. "Do any of your friends at school ever talk about their fathers?" I thought about it for a minute, and answered" No, Daddy". I didn't realize it before, because I was naïve and took for granted that families were just like mine. It became a sobering thought for me even as a kid. I could count on one hand how many of my friends on the block I grew with who actually had their fathers in their home.

When my daughters were born, I wanted to give them what my father and mother gave to me; even though their mother and I didn't see eye to eye. My mom and dad worked together to raise me, and I was determined to raise my kids the same way. It didn't matter whether I was married to the mother or not, my kids were going to get the best of what I could offer. I've seen relationships in my youth and over the years where the parents used their children as pawns and objects based on whatever took place in their relationship. I was not raised that way, and I refused to subject my children to that either. My relationship with their mother would never be a deciding factor on how I treat my children. I knew I would always be a part of their lives, and do what was best for them. I saw my parents making sacrifices, and that's how I was raised. I truly believe that you make sacrifices for the people you love and care about.

When I think about sacrifices, even contributing to this book was a huge one for me. I am not much of a talker, and I certainly don't share much about me personally. I was glad to be asked.

Although in the beginning, I didn't feel I had much to add. As a man, digging deep into my thoughts has been good. It helped me discover things I hadn't given full attention to until now. As I talked about earlier, when we deal with ourselves, it helps our children and the household overall. I didn't feel like I had much to offer but I believe this will help somebody.

I've done some things for love, and like most, my heart has been broken in the past. I have learned from it. I try not to make the same mistakes and avoid allowing women with the same personality traits back in my life. I was young when I experienced that first heartache, but back then I had a certain invincibility accompanied with a bit of arrogance and ignorance. I believed that whatever we want to do will be accomplished by just saying it alone. Working through the pain of my broken heart was difficult, but I didn't let it deter me from loving other people. You know, it was a learning tool. Love is like any other area of your life, when something doesn't go your way; you don't just give up on it.

An ugly relationship may try to mess you up by giving you a bad disposition about moving forward. It may cause you to treat the next person wrong if you are not aware of the effects. I pay attention to what women say and do when I'm engaging with them. There have been times when I had to say "don't blame me for what the last man did to you before I came along." I try my best not to do that as well. I can't compare her to the previous relationship where that woman did the same thing. We have to give each other the benefit of the doubt.

Chapter Seven

MY PURPOSE DEFINED

A great woman understands within herself that she is no longer just a good woman. It is because she has endured many trials and tests that have caused her eyes to be opened to life matters that have clearly defined her purpose and greatness. The whole point of this developmental process is for her to stand in her own authenticity while discovering her true self in the midst of struggles and challenges. Based upon these challenges, a great woman endures to acquire the understanding that she carries *perfect love that casteth out fear*. (I John 4:18)

While God is revealing to her about the enemies of the great man, she possesses the power to war and skillfully comfort him. This power is called, "Dunamis." However, this revelation does not diminish her tests. The more she develops power and strength to stand in times of pressure, the more she is required to use it (Luke 12:48). When a great man becomes weary or troubled, she has the ability to bring peace to his soul. When he is angry, she has the power to calm his fears. She does this through prayer, as she stands in her own identity not allowing his issues to frustrate her or become her issues.

God reveals more regarding her distractive opponents, which causes her to continue in spiritual warfare. At this juncture, she is no longer emotionally moved by the enemies that attempt to attack her, or the great man in her life. She lives with a peace that surpasses all understanding, and it rests, rules and abides in her heart (Philippians 4:7). It doesn't matter what comes his way, or what she sees, because she is now confident that the power of God resides on the inside of her.

When the great man's emotions take him off course, this is the perfect time for her to govern hers. It is only during times of difficulties that a great woman learns how to manage her emotions, which empowers her to live by the fruit of the spirit: **love, joy, peace, forbearance, goodness, self-control, kindness, faithfulness**, and **gentleness**. (Galatians 5:22-23). Even when a man is angered, a great woman exhibits the fruit of the spirit. When he's continuously provoked to anger, her fruit is produced even the more. Every fruit is encompassed within the core called "Love (Agape)." Now, once that's been developed and worked on the inside of her, she has acquired a greater level of maturity. It is imminent that she will move forward, because God is revealing more to her about who she is. Not only is the adversary threatened by the great man, he's also threatened by the great woman who understands her divine purpose and true identity.

The great man maintains his authority at all times. When God presents the great woman to him, he possesses the mind of God to see her as himself. He needs her strength and power, because it was given for them to both authentically stand before Christ. The great woman understands that the success of the great man lies within her, and is very confident with this truth. She never loses her sense of self. The great woman will stand no matter what, in spite of how she feels, or what things look like. That's why the woman must be confident in who she is, as her purpose is being clearly defined. The enemy doesn't want them to realize their significance of being together. The devil doesn't know the revelation that God gives them.

The word of God enlightens us that Satan knows the written word (logos) of God, which simply means that he is only familiar with what is stated with fear and trembling (James 2:19). It is imperative that we keep in mind that Satan does not know the revelation (rhema) of God's word given by the Holy Spirit. That is why receiving revelation from His word is so important. It is what empowers us to have a personal relationship with God. However, I want to stress that the adversary doesn't want women to understand their revealed purpose and identity, as being great! Women, when we no longer vacillate or are unstable in our emotions, and the revelation is implemented in our lives, the demise of the enemies' tactics is a done deal!

Women, no matter where you are at this juncture of your life or what is transpiring, I want to esteem you as a great woman. Within the core of our being, we have been given a great deal of substance. Please be assured that the enemy is intimidated by your power and strength, which makes it difficult for him to convince you to go astray from your purpose. We stand against all odds! Regardless of our innate ability to make our own way in life, God's original intent for His creation; man and woman will never change. We will see the wholesome effects for His plan, as our lives are aligned accordingly.

We, great women, are life givers and world changers. It is necessary for us to witness the fruit of our labor in every aspect of life, including the great man!

GREAT MAN WHERE ART THOU?

The Silent Cry of a Woman's Heart...

AGE: 54
STATUS: MARRIED
RESIDE: PENSACOLA, FLORIDA

I believe it is hard to be a great man today. We are out here, but we're not stand-outs. A great man is not looking to be patted on the back; selfish ambition does not drive him. He's not looking to be recognized or given accolades. A pedestal is not important to him. He doesn't need someone to push or motivate him. As a matter of fact, he understands that at times he must be willing to stand alone. It is not easy to be a great man. He is not jockeying for position, status or material things. He is committed and willing to doing whatever needs to be done. Whether the work is dirty or hard or whether he is hated by others, which he often is, he remains committed. A great man, by some stretches of the imagination would probably be considered a chauvinist. In this day and age, he is going to govern himself by principals and standards which may seem old and staunch. I consider myself to be a gentleman, and at the same time I demand to be respected. I am going to walk in respect of myself, as well as others.

Family is huge to me, which is why I take the responsibility of fatherhood very serious. When I was 15 years old, a relative of ours came to my parent's home. I was a pretty popular kid in school, and was well liked by many of my classmates and peers. Because of this, one of my uncles wanted me to start selling dope. We were standing in the front yard, and he was showing me these pills. I was scared to death! I was thinking what am I supposed to do? This is a grown man? I'm like, "Oh God, this is the first time I've ever been approached, and its family!" I was looking over my shoulder for someone to help me; and my mother could tell that something was wrong. She told my father, and he went down to my uncle's house, and told him, "If you ever show up at my house or come near my kids again, I promise, I'll kill you!"

Now, I'm not putting my emphasis on the incident or outcome. However, as a 15-year-old young man, I knew from then on without question, in spite of everything else my father would protect us with his life. It's one thing to hear or read about something like that, but it is something entirely different to have lived it. I knew from that moment that my dad loved us more than anything on the face of the earth. I learned about sacrificing and the unconditional love that a father should have for his children. He has a willingness to give of himself to protect and provide for them. That experience causes me to aspire to always do the same for my children. I'll never forget that moment.

The family is about the man, the children; but also about the great woman. I would think that every great woman wants a great man. However, here's where the problem comes in today: having a great man in your life comes with a price. He has a target on his back, his head and his life. Not just any woman can walk with that type of man. She, without question, has to be a praying woman. She must be tenacious herself. If the devil can't get him directly, he will attempt to come at him through her. She has got to be spiritually wise and mature enough to withstand the darts for that great man. She has to warfare for that great man just as much as she wants to love him. She will have to understand that in walking alongside him, it's not primarily about her vision. Most of the time, the very purpose for her life is going to be in that man and she must be willing to yield to that. She will have to come out of the forefront and allow him to be the great man.

A lot of women will say they want a great man, but will fight against him tooth and nail. We live in a society where everyone wants to know what's in it for them. If the great man is a godly man (who he should be), the last thing she has to worry about is if she will be blessed in the end. I am reminded of Boaz in the bible. If a woman wants a Boaz in her life, she has to humble herself and lay at his feet. She must know that God's will and objective for her to be in the great man's life is for her to be his helpmeet. In other words, she has to be confident that she is the one for him. If she does not yield to this perspective, the great man will be constantly distracted by her wants and worldly views.

This is a tall order for the great man and woman, and sometimes in our haste and impatience, we try to help God out and make the choices. Many of us have made this mistake over and over, and our hearts have been broken. Before meeting my wife, I certainly experienced heartache. I needed healing for my heart, but also healing from the past relationships. Too many of us rebound immediately after the break up without giving ourselves any time for healing or deliverance. We don't spend time before the Lord himself in prayer to seek what should and shouldn't be. Look, I had to tell the Lord that I could no longer do it on my own. I could not take the failure of another relationship. I needed God's guidance like never before. I knew my life had to line up as a life of sacrifice for my wife, as well as my children. I knew I could not just be that for any woman. She had to be that woman God placed in my life. My healing process took a year and a half.

Chapter Eight

I Know Who I AM...

Too often, we as women are so busy thinking about the needs of a man that unknowingly we become prey to the enemies' devices within his soul. God never intended for us to be positioned in the lives of men to lose ourselves. We have to first learn how to stand in our own authenticity. God deemed us worthy to walk in His fullness when He created us as "Woman." Every day we are given breathe in our bodies, we strive to be good or great, but we need to discover who we truly are before we put an adjective on it. Understanding ourselves as a "Woman" is our first priority. We must maintain the "Woman" without allowing our various roles to smother and suffocate her. Our responsibility above all is to be the woman God created and developed us to be; the key word being *developed*.

Instantaneously, you don't just fully mature. The formation of breasts, hips, legs, and physical stature do not constitute our internal progression as women. Many of us are stuck as little girls;

underdeveloped females on the inside, due to our past emotional pains. As women, when we are emotionally unhealed in our damaged places we may end up settling for any type of man versus a great one. In this case, we often experience more abuse in various ways. There are great men of all ages in our lives, beginning with our fathers. Each one of them has been assigned to contribute to our development. Unfortunately, this may have been stifled by the absence, abuse or stagnation of our fathers which hinders our process. Healing must occur in order to fully embrace the other great men God placed in our lives. In order to do so, God must reveal to us the purpose of our maternal and paternal lineage, and who we are before we can live effectively.

Women, it is so important that we take a really good look at ourselves before even giving thought to the great man. There is a process of preparation we all must go through to transform our hearts and minds. Unfortunately, we have become products of our environment which shaped our thinking, and robbed us from our true selves. As great women, our warfare starts by taking our power back to create and produce. We must stand with the great man to build a legacy for future generational leaders. I believe that a woman should understand her greatness, and the power she possesses prior to being presented to the great man. A great man is cognizant of the fact that the power (dunamis) endowed within is not solely for her. Primarily, it was given to her for him. I firmly believe that God strategically did this to keep reminding him that he cannot accomplish greatness on his own. It is not good for the great man to be alone.

The great man transcends from working on his major issues to working on his mission. He is operating as a man with a plan; and that type of man should not be alone according to God's word (Genesis 2:18). A great man knows who he is and whose he is. So, when God has given him a woman to walk beside him, he understands that she is there to assist him in his mission and to meet the needs of the vision at all cost. She is there to work with him, not against him. Moreover, she gratifies him with all his pleasurable desires, and have fun doing so. Her power is very important, because she is the womb of man. Her womb was given to carry his legacy.

In order for her to handle this substance and power, she must have the ability to handle his emotional agony (not abuse) in spite of the discomfort. There are certain things in life that the great man was not emotionally equipped to handle. The great man is not a weak man. He has difficulties managing his emotions, because his mind is so powerful. When distractions attempt to deter his thinking, the brunt is given to the woman, because she can handle insurmountable levels of agony. As a result, she does not harbor it, but she gives it back to God through travail. With an attentive ear, her Heavenly Father immediately takes heed to her silent cry on behalf of herself, as well as that great man.

The great woman must keep believing in the men in her life; father, husband, son, brother, uncle, nephew, etc., while they are being transformed from good to great. She continuously fights the good fight of faith to prevent her hope from being deferred. Everything in life must go through a process, including her own self-growth and development.

As a spiritual leader, one of the revelations I have received and teach is that women are attracted to men like their fathers. Not many people understand this spiritual principle, because it is a mystery. That is why the great woman must have a relationship with Christ, so the Holy Spirit can reveal. Her revelation should be synonymous with what her mother should have told her concerning her father;

only for the strongholds of the great man to be continuously annihilated through warfare. If she looks at the fight of her mother concerning her father, knowingly or unknowingly, she will find herself looking in the mirror.

Whether the father was present or absent in her life, it does not negate or diminish her fight. However, if she doesn't know of the spiritual forces she is wrestling with, it will deplete her, if not destroy her. As a result, a woman is enticed by the spiritual forces (good and evil) operating through the lineage of her father as well. The great woman can become weary while walking in her greatness.

Let me give you a scenario that I hope will paint a clear picture of the importance of knowing our true identity as the great woman, and the reason it is important to understand why oppositions will come against you. My example is based upon Apostle Paul's letter in Ephesians, Chapter 6. The church of Ephesus is characterized as a mature (great) church. They did not despise instruction, and went through processes to grow and understand their roles and assignment as men and women.

In the very beginning of this chapter, Paul wastes no time in giving instructions. He tells the children to obey their parents in the Lord (verse 1) and admonishes fathers not to provoke their children to wrath (anger). He goes on to speak to the servants in the house as well. Why is this important? Because of mission and vision; the great man and woman have many responsibilities that can't be accomplished without a team. They need the assistance of trusted people to execute the plans for continued growth while maintaining the wealth (resources) that have already been obtained within their home and business. In addition to the family, the servants are also benefactors of the great man's inheritance.

The great man is not a struggling and broke man. However, he can experience financial challenges at different times in his life. He may not begin with a lot, but he doesn't remain there because he follows spiritual principles that bring his family and legacy increase and expansion.

So, we hear clearly the instructions given to the children, the servants, as well as the father. What about the great woman (mother)? The mother was not omitted, because she was given her commands in the book of Genesis (the beginning) when God put enmity between her and the serpent (enemy). As you continue to read Ephesians 6, there is now a better understanding about the "WE" that is wrestling not against flesh and blood (verse 12). It's the family; husband, wife, children as well as the servants. The legacy was given to the entire household. The womb bearer (woman) has been assigned to fight and wrestle with a subtle beast (serpent). This is done on behalf of her legacy and based on her position. The great woman has hostility against her enemy, and she has been given the power and authority in Christ Jesus to bruise his head, and annihilate his wiles and schemes. What woman will sit back and see her family destroyed? Not the great woman! Revelations are not given to the great man concerning some household matters, when the great woman is in place to defend and wage war against his enemies.

Circumstances will come and try to divide an established household, but the great man and great woman standing united learns how to handle them skillfully. This is not from a physical standpoint, but a spiritual one. The Holy Spirit has a responsibility to reveal to the great woman on behalf of the great man. God speaks to the great man about what he is supposed to do, as he seeks and hears the voice of God for instructions to build their legacy. However, the great woman seeks the revelation of God for their family. They both get the same information, but it's channeled differently.

If more men and women understood their roles and kept their stance, we would see less crime, alcoholism, drug abuse, perversion, and other deficits we are experiencing in our homes, communities, and churches. That's why we see so many tragedies such as; killings, murder, rape, etc. Some men are utilizing what God has rightfully given them for evil and not for good. God has given a righteous anger to great men to make things happen, and they must understand that they have to protect and provide for their women (wives) and children.

Their hearts pound with powerful thoughts such as: *"It's up to me to make things happen for my family!"* Within their speech you will hear the indignation within their souls due to a righteous anger that causes them to stand in their authority and dominion. They stand and nothing is going to make them bow down to anyone, including the women in their lives. They are building as God has instructed. They are not only providing for their families, but for generations to come. Great men stand collectively; not just as one man, but a nation!

The great woman needs the great man for his strength and powerful mind, as opposed to his material gains. She will speak to him based upon who he is, beyond what she sees and what he already knows about himself. Because those heartfelt words may be foreign to him, it could first ignite his fear? The great man has to have uplifting words deposited in his heart, because somewhere in his past, pieces of his soul has been broken and fragmented. This is inevitable. The great woman speaks life to make those places whole. It's only because God is revealing to her and showing her truth. She has no ulterior motives. She just knows who she is and what she comes to add to his life. It's nothing she has to work at or prepare for, it's all she knows. Her life is warfare; intercession and being in God's presence. He has a responsibility to receive it, and allow God to work in him and on him. After she prays, it's between him and God. The great woman knows how to LET GO, and LET GOD concerning every situation. She acquires wisdom and skillset to speak to him about what has been revealed in its proper time. The men have a responsibility to allow God to germinate the words in their soul, for continual architectural design of His workmanship.

Everything God takes us through transitions us into greatness. You can't have it by yourself. You have it together with another person or people; greatness is not a solo act. We're always going through processes from good to great. When we are transitioning, often we are challenged to get stuck on good when God is to taking us to great places. However, this requires more responsibility and commitment. Luke 12:47

The great man and woman endures many trials and tribulations before experiencing His greatness. When God was ready to propel the men and women of Israel to their destiny, He told Moses to tell Pharaoh that "I AM" sent you; *I AM THAT I AM* (Exodus 3:14). At that point, He was ready to manifest Himself as *GREAT!* He was good to the Israelites when He kept them. He was good because He didn't allow them to die. He was good when He sent them a deliverer. But the GREAT God opened up the sea, and showed His signs and wonders that His people may be free. God reveals His true self to great people when He is ready to move on their behalf.

Are you willing to acknowledge who you truly are so that your children, grandchildren, and great-grandchildren can be free? It's time to come out of denial and open our eyes to truth. In this era of time which we live, the Great I AM is ready to manifest himself through every great woman who embraces her true identity and proclaim, I AM A... Dunamis Woman. We are women of power fashioned and built for the healing, deliverance and freedom for the great men in our lives.

GREAT MAN WHERE ART THOU?

The Silent Cry of a Woman's Heart...

AGE: 48
STATUS: DIVORCED
RESIDE: LEMONT, IL

Where are the great men? That is a good question, because most of the great men who I knew are no longer on this planet. It is hard to find them. They are the ones you typically don't see because they work behind the scenes. Most great men don't let others know they are great. However, when you truly know them you realize this quality is displayed consistently. Their greatness is the depth of what they are willing to give without any expectation of receiving. The greatest men I currently know are servant leaders, who have no voice for their accomplishments. They don't speak or talk about it, they just give.

I am a man, so I know how we typically isolate ourselves. Because of this, we tend to think or act like we live on these individual islands created by us. Without drawing us back into a world where life is about more than just us, women tend to let us go. It may be a "man's world", but definitely not a man's island. I believe women have an influence that can bring us out. When a woman is confident, she will connect with him, and guide him back to a place of reality instead of feeling defeated and giving up. We (men and women) need each other.

I take fatherhood seriously because I loved kids even when I was young and without any. I want to teach kids and I genuinely enjoy being around them. Most of all, my father was an absentee parent, so I want to show my children what a father should be.

In order to handle my broken heart, I had to touch that brokenness; I embraced my damaged places. As I tried to ignore the pain, or go on with life without addressing it, I wasn't able to function. I had to reach in and not only deal with the broken heart experience of that moment, but deal with all the issues. I had to revisit all the times my heart was broken prior, bringing the past into the present so I could recreate my future.

Chapter Nine

A WARRIOR AT HEART

Every woman must embark upon a place of understanding where she realizes that her silent cry is her warfare, as well as her worship. The internal wrestling is never between man and woman, but the battle is between her and the *opponents of the great men* assigned to her life. It is not the relationships between her and the great men that are at stake, but their legacy as a whole. What I am telling you is not based upon the natural realm we see. The great woman must learn spiritual principles based upon the Word of Truth that empowers her to fight and win in the Spirit. Every woman holds the men in her life dear to her heart. The enemy seeks after a woman's heart to weaken her so her fight is ineffective. When men are displaced from her life she feels the void, and this is her silent cry. I have come to discover this myself, which is from not always having the opportunity to be loved, heard, regarded and appreciated by the great man, my father. This is what makes me a warrior at heart.

The word of God backs this up in Genesis 3:15 when it talks about the enmity between the woman and the serpent. God put hostility (anger) there because the woman has the ability to bear down, endure, and wrestle (pray) on behalf of great men. The great woman understands that it's about her excellence, which will only be seen when she is positioned for purpose. This is the reason for the warfare.

It is unfortunate that many of us don't understand what's being conveyed here. We are becoming ensued in spiritual battles, and are being defeated due to lack of understanding. Our homes, families and communities are steadily growing worse or being destroyed because, we, the womb bearers, have become independent and proud in our own accomplishments. However, one of the most powerful things the great woman can accomplish is the building up of great men. When the great man has experienced brokenness, the great woman can handle it to draw him closer to His Creator. She must become spiritually sound, and endure her own process of emotional healing for spiritual maturation to see outcomes.

We must first understand who we are as women. We must be very clear on our position and posture. When those elements are in place, then more revelation will come. God will expose things to that great woman regarding the great men in her life, so she is aware of the schemes and tactics the enemy brings their way. However, having information without the proper application of warfare will not produce the results necessary. We need to have keen discernment, which gives us information for intercession that produces outcomes, exploits, miracles, signs and wonders. I am a living witness!

Women, our warfare is proactive for the things great men will experience that attempt to frustrate the plans and purposes of God. For instance, a great man hears the voice of God, giving him explicit instructions. As he follows directives, his oppositions will be revealed to the great woman for warfare. She stays in her position understanding that she is the "womb bearer". She stands boldly and in her authority. That's why in Ephesians 6:18, Paul says pray always with supplication; and when you've done all you can do to withstand, stand!

As great women, we have to be situated in the lives of great men, so we are entrusted with their hearts. We have to actively listen to what is being said but more so what is not being conveyed. The silent cry of the great man is what is not being spoken. It can be hidden within his circumstances, anger, inadequacy or fear, just to name a few. It is those unspoken words that draws the heart of the great woman to his, to yield a harvest of healing, comfort and assurance. We take what we've heard with our hearts to God in prayer bearing our souls on behalf of great men. In conjunction, we take the insight given by God, in its proper timing, and communicate it to the great men in our lives. We encourage them to continue to withstand when they've done all to stand.

You don't ever give up on great men, but you stand as a warrior! Your stance is an indicator that your mind and emotions are fortified to what you believe. When great men are in your life, more is required of you, the great woman. Her life of prayer and worship has to be keen and profound. She must be disciplined and consistent in her walk with Christ. We have to always be prepared for what's to come through intentional living. It must be our lifestyle, because great men have so much to conquer and produce. The goal of the enemy is to destroy every great man and his legacy, but with a great woman that will not occur as long as she continues to fight spiritually. She is a confident warrior and worshipper who knows how to stand in the gap.

Every warrior is aware that it takes a host of women; two or more to win the war. The enemies of a great man never give up. Therefore, as great women, we must remain united without fear of exposing our wounds and becoming vulnerable with one another. This requires us to trust. Personally, I understand this is easier said than done. However, it is necessary because of our families and children are at stake. Women, I admonish us to stop fighting one another, and see the real enemy for who he is and what he is endeavoring to do; steal, kill and destroy. Begin to gather the great women in your midst to come together to pray for our great men while revealing our hearts.

GREAT MAN WHERE ART THOU?

The Silent Cry of a Woman's Heart...

AGE: 44
STATUS: SEPARATED
RESIDE: SAN JOSE, CALIFORNIA

I believe the great men are out there, and they are honestly overlooked. They are in every area and walk of life. They are the men who refuse to quit no matter of their circumstance. They are the men who refuse to let situations change their character or who they are. They are not always the Vice President or CEO, sometimes they are just that father who will show up to every one of their kid's games or do homework with them. He is the man who will do everything to make sure that his children respect their mother. He is also that man who will break down at times. He would rather do it in front of the person whom he loves; or with people who will allow him the freedom to express his emotions.

Sometimes a great man is a silent one. What keeps him silent is the strength he uses to keep people confident in his greatness (including himself), even when he appears to be looking less than strong in the eyes of others. A great man can be strong and at the same time very weak. His weakness will be misunderstood by others, yet he is still great. They are the ones who will take a stand and speak up when others won't.

A woman of power must truly understand what she possesses when she is with that man who has chosen her to be with him. She has the influence to give him strength, and at the same time has the ability to tear him down to nothing. A woman of power must recognize when that man really wants to be vulnerable, but hasn't broken through that layer yet where he can be unguarded in front of her. She must know that a man can be weak, and she needs to understand this to avoid being the one that crushes him completely. That is the life lesson I have learned, and I can teach others about it.

I chose to take my responsibilities as a father, because mine was absent in my upbringing. I was determined, no matter the circumstance, to break that trend and be a part of my children's lives. I wanted to hear them call me "Daddy," and I speak to them as their father. For me, it is breaking a pattern that was set in my own childhood, and no matter what people say, children need their father. He can teach his child things that a mother cannot and will not ever understand. A father's role is to impart into his children and protect them. I choose to always be with my kids no matter what, because when I was younger I was hurt by a family member. It affected me for a number of years, probably well into my thirties. I wonder sometimes what would have happened had my father been there. I never want my children to experience that sense of abandonment and not feeling safe. I choose to be loyal to my children, regardless of how challenging situations may become.

I handle a broken heart by waking up every morning. Despite what I'm going through, I wake up and ask for forgiveness. Sometimes, those warning signs I missed start popping in my head. I asked for forgiveness for trying to be so much of a "man" that I blinded myself to the problems that were happening. I thought I could handle everything on my own, and as a "man" I was supposed to have absolute confidence all the time. I admit to failing, but I don't see myself as a failure.

I will say this to men, "Do everything possible to get back up, whether that is through prayer or realizing when opportunities come that will help you rebuild and restore yourself. Sometimes women don't know that they're breaking your heart. You should begin to understand how broken you were even before getting into another relationship. Take it step by step to rebuild yourself. You will come out stronger. Never see yourself as a failure! The thoughts will come, but don't hold on to them." When experiencing a broken heart, don't believe all is lost. Deal with it by admitting that you're broken, and forgiving yourself, and others involved. Truly make sure you heal emotionally and spiritually. I do this through prayer and through writing. Whatever it is that helps you with your healing; pour into it and you'll end up being better.

Chapter Ten

TRUE LOVE WILL FIND YOU

True love is not limited to the involvement of the great man and great woman; it is expressed in many ways and forms. All true love stems from Christ' love for us, and we embody that love and share it with others. But for the sake of this chapter, we will explore the love relationship of the great man and great woman for a meaningful understanding towards the depth of that love.

I wholeheartedly believe that true love finds us, and that we don't have to seek it out. Proverbs 18:22 substantiates my claim. As women, we want, and literally need that love. When I speak of true love, I'm not speaking from a romantic (eros), brotherly (phileo) or parental (storge) perspective (you may want to research those on your own). I'm referring to a selfless love (agape). A kind of love that exudes from your body, soul and spirit, because all three entities have been committed to Christ, Our Lord. Usually when a discussion is taking place about agape, it is limited to the fact that it is unconditional love, but it actually goes deeper. Agape love should make a statement, a declaration from the great man to the great woman pertaining to the height, length and depth and endurance of this love. It says "If I never get anything from you in return, I will still give unto you. If I'm not getting all the sex I want, I still commit to you. When I don't have feel-good moments with you, I will always regard you. If you don't meet my pleasurable needs, I shall find pleasure in you. If you're not cooking, cleaning and caring for me, I'll always do and care for you!" Now, that is a LOVE like no other!

Much of the love that is shared these days comes with conditions, and is more erotic in nature. You rub my back; I rub yours. You do for me; I do for you. Many women are giving their bodies away, misconstruing sex as love. Just because you have sex, doesn't mean that you are being loved. Erotic feelings keep you longing for more and more.

Agape love can find you in one or any combination of these states: broken, hurting, isolated, lonely, rejected, abandoned, bruised, wounded, and/or abused. In these broken places, God's love hears a woman's heart, which is her silent cry. In response, He sends the assigned great man for her life. He restores her soul. Restoration is also needed for the great man, because he has issues and infirmities as well. Remember, without each other both are incomplete and both need one another.

It is a false perception that the great man will ride in as a knight in shining armor on a white horse to rescue you from your financial distress. His search is for agape also, looking for that in return from the great woman. Far too much time and energy is wasted looking for a man based on what he can do for you. The great man just wants to know if you can love him for who he is and not for what he possesses. In our developmental process, God poses the same question to us: "If I never give you another tangible thing, can you love Me for Who I am? Will you love Me in your distress? If your body is wracked with pain, will you serve Me? If you're left standing alone, will you trust Me?" When the great man understands the love of God, he asks the same type of questions.

Initially, these questions may not be verbally asked by the great man. However, there is a testing period that the great woman goes through for her heart to be proven and revealed. The great man wants to be assured that this kind of woman has his back, and have the ability to cherish his heart. God takes you through a refining process, so once you are in the presence of the great man, you will be equipped to handle his test.

It is similar to when we are in school; there are quizzes, tests, midterms and finals. I loved quizzes because they were short, and usually pretty easy to pass. Tests and midterms are a little more extensive, and they include information that was already learned. However, the final exam includes the most questions to answer with equations to solve. Each tier of testing is designed to prove that you know the material and subject matter thoroughly to go to the next level. In the spiritual realm, there is no chronological time frame to how information and answers comes for your destiny. The great man assigned to your life will look to see how you handle each test to prove that you are the great woman assigned to him.

God presents the great man to you, because He seeks him out just for you. Before the great man takes you as his wife, you must take the final exam of him testing your heart. That is why the great man will test your heart to ensure that you are the one he was seeking for. When making his assessment and evaluation, he looks beyond your outward beauty. The great man doesn't make your outward appearance his main priority. Of course, he will be visually stimulated, but what he's really examining is your inner workings. He is also testing your character, observing how you handle your family, finances and friends. He's observing how you interact with people in general. He pays attention to how you face life's circumstances and challenges, and how you are fighting to make your dreams a reality.

He watches how you handle your personal affairs. He's taking note of how you make decisions, and how you follow through on the ones you make. In many cases, he is noticing all these areas quietly and discreetly. There are times that he may speak on it, and it may seem like criticism. In actuality, he also wants to see how you handle constructive feedback. He is determining if you remain in a posture of maturity without becoming offended. It may even feel like he's being condescending, but he's observing what type of pressure you can handle.

As the great woman, you are incredibly valuable to him. Confidently, you must remain assured. The great man doesn't need to have a lot of women surrounding him. As a matter of fact, he won't because there aren't many who are willing to go through the process. The great woman is able to sustain when she is upheld by a host of great women who stand faithful and true with her.

The great man observes the relationship you have with other women in your circle. He wants to see if you gossip with them. He's listening to determine if you're telling his business. Oh my God, they cannot stand for you to do that! His thoughts are private. When he shares them with you he wants to trust and know that they are not being shared with anyone else. He will also subtly test your inner circle to ensure that you are not telling his business. Remember, the great woman cherishes his heart. Therefore, she will not share his innermost secrets. The great man will take one step forward, but if he sees something he deems questionable he'll take a few steps back. He won't leave your life because he sees your greatness. The great woman's primary focus is to stay true to God, and herself. This is key. When those areas are aligned, the relationship with the great man will follow suit.

Do not become discouraged or distressed thinking about the testing period. It does not require you to work to show something, it is not a proving based on duties. Proving is not about defending yourself, or being on edge. Most times, you won't have to say a word. It's really just about being you, the Dunamis Woman; woman of power that you are. Continue to be that mother, daughter, friend, leader, servant, talent and treasure that you are. Continue to be faithful unto God, which is your first priority. That is the acceptable will of God for your life. Luke 12:47 touches on what the Master requires, based on what we've been given. It is God who's putting the demands on you, through the great man, because you do not possess mediocre power! Literally, this kind of power (dunamis) change lives, circumstances, situations and make the impossible possible. It is the same resurrection power that is in Jesus, and it was given to all mankind. God took us out of man and created and fashioned every woman, knowing that a great man would need her.

Let this serve as encouragement to you: Honey, just be who you are! True love; agape will seek you out and find you. Just be yourself! Allow yourself every opportunity to cultivate and grow your garden of greatness, and you will reap the harvest intended for you. We, as women, can't get ahead of ourselves. Sometimes we get impatient, and we want what we want, and we want it yesterday. Every testing period must be endured. The proving and refining fire of God; The Father, as well as the testing of your heart of the great man is inevitable. Each test reveals your genuine and authentic greatness. The trials bring forth all that you are, and you are amazing. God knows when you're ready for His love (agape).

The main component you will need to get you through every test and trial is nothing but your worship. Worship is a matter of the heart. You don't have to come any certain way or you don't have to be all together lovely. You don't have to fluently know and recite scriptures, or defend your case or cause. God sees you, knows you, and loves you right where you are and for whom you are. His grace is sufficient. God will do the miraculous in your life, as you continue to humble yourself. Humility creates an altar upon the tablets of your heart for God to do an amazing work in your life. The Father replenishes you, increases your strengths and gives you strategies to succeed and overcome.

When I think of all that Our Father has done for me, as well as how He protects and provides for me it, causes tears to stream down my face. There is such a peace He has given me, even in times of trials and testing. That is solely based on the relationship I have with Him. As great women, we must always remember that we are daughters of the Most High. We should always have a heart of gratitude for the very miniscule things in life. We take that same heart of worship even while being tested, and walk in a greater peace and joy. We must know and understand that all things work together for our good, including every interaction with the great man. Because of God's unfailing love, the love of the great man compliments what He has already provided. So, rest assured that true love is waiting for you and will find you.

GREAT MAN WHERE ART THOU?

The Silent Cry of a Woman's Heart...

WARFARE PRAYER
HISTORICAL PERSPECTIVE

Jeremiah 9 speaks about how a nation refused to acknowledge God, turned against His ways and lived by their own thoughts, laws, and rules. They became full of pride and forgot who they were; made in His likeness and image. Jeremiah 9:17-18 specifically shows us a strategy to bring attention to the ruin that was plaguing the land. The Lord says "Consider now! Call for the wailing women to come; send for the most skillful of them. [18] Let them come quickly and wail over us till our eyes overflow with tears and water streams from our eyelids.

Look around you! Do you see the destruction in our families, communities and nations? Do you recognize the pride, disobedience and haughtiness that have come upon God's people in this day and age? The hour is now and God is beckoning the wailing women (great women), to come forth and travail on behalf of our men, families, communities and the nations.

Throughout history, women have been at the forefront of religious, cultural, political, economic and social change in the world, through prayer. There is no major change that has happened on a large and significant scale without prayer. For example, since the early 1800s, groups of women from various denominations (Presbyterian, Methodist, Baptist, etc.) have come together to engage in communal prayer, as it relates to mission work to the nations.

During slavery, communal prayer and the gathering of slaves was outlawed on most plantations. However, the desire to pray for change was so strong that the slaves devised techniques to avoid being caught at these meetings. They often met in woods, thickets, ravines and even gullies. They would wet quilts and rags or kneel and pray into vessels of water to keep their voices from penetrating the air. It is noted that even Harriet Tubman recognized the power of prayer for change, which was monumental in her decision to be free.

In 1948, as a result of the post-European war, the European Baptist Women's Union was birthed. Several women (American and European) gathered in a hotel foyer, holding hands and praying John 3:16 in their own language. To this day, women gather together for a Day of Prayer. It is noted that women travel miles, and swim across rivers to reach the place of the prayer gatherings.

The end of the civil war in Liberia is a more recent example of how when women come together in prayer and travail on behalf of the nations, change is inevitable. In 2003, a movement to protest war was led by Leymah Gbowee. She not only gathered Christian women, but women of all faiths and religions including Muslims, to show solidarity through prayer. Within two years, they succeeded in ending the country's civil war and brought peace to their nation.

Throughout the bible and world history, prayer has been at the forefront of change. It is not by happenstance that in 1 Thessalonians 5:17 the Word admonishes us to pray without ceasing because we are yet again in the time and season that we are open to destruction. Once more God is beckoning us as women to not just pray but engage in spiritual warfare on behalf of our men, families, communities and nations.

We end this book in prayer. In everything that you learned and will apply once you put this book down, prayer must be at the helm of your transition from good to great and from great to greater.

GREAT MAN WHERE ART THOU?

The Silent Cry of a Woman's Heart...

Father, In the Name of Jesus, we glorify You, because there's none other like You. No one compares to You; Your faithfulness, sovereignty, divinity, or loyalty. We worship You because of who You are. We thank You for being mindful of us. What is man that thou are mindful of him; and the son of man that thou visit him?

We thank You that You've made man a little lower than Your angels. We glorify You because You had an idea in mind when we were created. Not only did You have an idea, but You spoke and brought that idea to life when You said, "Let us make man in our image and in our likeness." We thank You that You also put the man to sleep, took a rib from him and formed woman. The rib was taken straight from his heart, and You used it to beautify woman.

You fashioned us as woman, took the substance that was in man, and put it deep down on the inside of us. You gave us strength through that substance: a fortitude and ability to endure with a power to produce miracles. Thank You for fearfully and skillfully creating us with a reproductive system so that we are able to produce and reproduce. This system is so strong and so miraculous that we are able to birth sons and daughters in the earth, and also birth men spiritually into their place of destiny, purpose and power. We thank You for being able to endure the pains of labor as women, all the contractions and circumstances that comes with the birthing process. I thank You that our bodies are able expand in order to bring forth life in various sizes, shapes and personalities. Thank You for creating each woman to birth, including those who have not conceived children in the natural. By Your Spirit, we can produce and reproduce spiritually, as well as naturally. That's just how powerful You designed us.

I thank You for choosing each and every woman on this earth to be here, and that You sent us equipped. You endowed us with wisdom that no educational system can provide. Governmental assistance may be a temporary resource, but You are the True Source. There's no religion or doctrinal view of man that can teach us, there's no managed care medical system that can provide the nourishment or the aid that we need beyond Your healing power. There is no paycheck on our job, or corporate system that can give us the reward of our labor; only You as Our Manufacturer. You created us, which give us guarantee that if we follow Your plans and live by Your purpose, that we will prosper as Your legal agents in the earth. You've given us everything we need on the inside for success.

Thank You for creating us to be powerful women who have a mandate and a mantle to come together and create change. I thank You that every woman I have met in my life has ability and supernatural strength. I call them forth, in Jesus Name, that we may stand united for our sons, husbands, brothers, uncles, and the men who we encounter in business and wherever we go. The cry of our hearts is that we need them in our homes, communities, the workplace, and in the presence of God. We need our men to worship You, and You alone. We need them to be properly positioned in our lives. We need them to appreciate the power we possess to maintain our homes, families and communities. In the Name of Jesus, I call forth warring women to stand together, as agents of change.

I take authority over every spirit of dissension, competition, jealousy and betrayal that wants to operate in us as women. I speak loyalty! I speak life! I speak commitment! I speak dedication! I speak faithfulness to one another! God, I decree that we will be united in these latter days and era of time. Bring us together by Your spirit and join our hearts that we may see as one with no division. Bind us in love and faith that we may be able to wail on behalf of our men with one mind.

Not as a reactive measure, but proactively so our sons and daughters may continuously be healed. God, let us come together as women that we may bring healing to the hearts of each other so that our children may be impacted. We pray now so that in the future our sons will attract the wives of their youth who will be faithful to them. We pray also that our daughters have husbands as reflection of Your likeness and image to protect and provide for their families.

Heal us and bring harmony that we may teach our daughters how to stand, wail, and to pray. We pray they will model what they see in us as mothers and women. I speak this over our lives, that they will not see competition, betrayal, dissension, envy and jealously because there shall be none. I thank You for unity among women of all races and nationalities; that we may empower and strengthen one another. I pray that we be midwives to each other when one woman is struggling. I pray we will stand united by her side to see her through to birth and deliver a healthy vision, dream and legacy for her children and future generations. We stand with her for every man that is in her life; that he may rise up to be the great man in the earth and take his proper position and occupancy. We pray the hearts of fathers be turned back to their children no matter how old they are.

Heavenly Father, we thank You that You honor us as daughters, and yet You see us as women who have developed in a state of maturity to execute Your plans, purpose ways and thoughts – not ours. Bring healing to our hearts as Your daughters. We need one another, and I thank You in advance and every woman who is reading this prayer and reading this book, let the healing begin with her. For every man who's reading this prayer and book, let the healing power of God overtake him, that he will see himself as a great man. Open our eyes to truth that we may fulfill purpose as women and men together.

We thank You in advance for every outcome, we thank You for change. We thank You for change in the atmosphere of our communities, homes and everywhere we go. We decree that every place that our feet tread upon has been changed and transformed for Your glory. Lift up our heads that we may look unto You. Open our ears so we can hear Your voice explicitly, that we may follow Your instructions. I pray that as we open our mouths and speak to other men and women, that life will be illuminated in their hearts.

In the Name of Our Lord and Savior, Jesus Christ I pray. Amen

WARFARE PRAYER
The Silent Cry of My Heart

As a great woman, I pray that this book has shifted your paradigm and ignited your heart to pray with power on purpose for the great men surrounding your life. They need you! However, when you have done all that you can do is when Our Father is ready to step in and move on our behalf. It's time to let go and let God. He is waiting to hear your heart. So, take a few minutes to write the silent cry of your heart. As you do so, please be assured that I stand united with you. I believe with you for every great man, young and old, to take their rightful position in the earth, as they seek the face of God and reside in His presence.

Matthew 18:19 (KJV) *Again I say unto you, That if two of you shall agree on earth as touching any thing that they shall ask, it shall be done for them of my Father which is in heaven.*

Heavenly Father,

_____
_____
_____
_____
_____
_____
_____
_____
_____
_____
_____
_____
_____
_____
_____
_____
_____
_____
_____
_____
_____
_____
_____

Ephesians 3:20-21 (KJV) *Now unto him that is able to do exceedingly abundantly above all that we ask or think, according to the power that worketh in us, 21 Unto him be glory in the church by Christ Jesus throughout all ages, world without end. Amen.*

APPENDIX: SCRIPTURE REFERENCES

DEDICATION

Psalm 91:16 (KJV)

With long life will I satisfy him, and shew him my salvation.

Psalm 37:23 (KJV)

The steps of a *good* man are ordered by the LORD: and he delighteth in his way

FOREWORD

Proverbs 31:10

Who can find a virtuous woman? for her price is far above rubies

1 Corinthians 2:4 (KJV)

And my speech and my preaching was not with enticing words of man's wisdom, but in demonstration of the Spirit and of power:

CHAPTER 1

Proverbs 18:22 (KJV)

Whoso findeth a wife findeth a good *thing*, and obtaineth favour of the LORD."

CHAPTER 2

1 Corinthians 11:3 (KJV)

"But I would have you know, that the head of every man is Christ; and the head of the woman *is* the man; and the head of Christ *is* God."

Genesis 2:22 (KJV)

"And the rib, which the LORD God had taken from man, made he a woman, and brought her unto the man."

CHAPTER 3

Genesis 12:1-2 (KJV)

1 Now the LORD had said unto Abram, Get thee out of thy country, and from thy kindred, and from thy father's house, unto a land that I will shew thee: 2 And I will make of thee a great nation, and I will bless thee, and make thy name great; and thou shalt be a blessing:

Genesis 11:28 (KJV)

And Haran died before his father Terah in the land of his nativity, in Ur of the Chaldees."

Genesis 17:6 (KJV)

⁶ And I will make thee exceeding fruitful, and I will make nations of thee, and kings shall come out of thee.

Genesis 17:16 (KJV)

And I will bless her, and give thee a son also of her: yea, I will bless her, and she shall be a mother of nations; kings of people shall be of her.

James 1:21 (KJV)

Wherefore lay apart all filthiness and superfluity of naughtiness, and receive with meekness the engrafted word, which is able to save your souls.

CHAPTER 4

Amos 3:3 (KJV)

"Can two walk together, except they be agreed?"

I Corinthians 14:33 (KJV)

For God is not the author of confusion, but of peace, as in all churches of the saints.

Proverbs 28:25 (KJV)

He that is of a proud heart stirreth up strife: but he that putteth his trust in the LORD shall be made fat.

Ecclesiastes 4:12 (KJV)

And if one prevail against him, two shall withstand him; and a threefold cord is not quickly broken

Proverbs 27:17 (KJV)

Iron sharpeneth iron; so a man sharpeneth the countenance of his friend

Proverbs 4:7 (KJV)

Wisdom *is* the principal thing; *therefore* get wisdom: and with all thy getting get understanding

CHAPTER 5

Genesis 15:1 (KJV)

After these things the word of the LORD came unto Abram in a vision, saying, Fear not, Abram: I *am* thy shield, *and* thy exceeding great reward

Ephesians 3:20 (KJV)

"Now unto him that is able to do exceeding abundantly above all that we ask or think, according to the power that worketh in us,"

Proverbs 31:1 (KJV)

The words of king Lemuel, the prophecy that his mother taught him.

Ephesians 6:12 (KJV)

"For we wrestle not against flesh and blood, but against principalities, against powers, against the rulers of the darkness of this world, against spiritual wickedness in high *places*."

Proverbs 18:24 (KJV)

"A man *that hath* friends must shew himself friendly: and there is a friend *that* sticketh closer than a brother."

Romans 1:18 (KJV)

For the wrath of God is revealed from heaven against all ungodliness and unrighteousness of men, who hold the truth in unrighteousness;"

Genesis 12:3 (KJV)

And I will bless them that bless thee, and curse him that curseth thee: and in thee shall all families of the earth be blessed."

Ephesians 5:33 (KJV)

"Nevertheless let every one of you in particular so love his wife even as himself; and the wife *see* that she reverence *her* husband."

CHAPTER 6

Proverbs 13:22 (KJV)

"A good *man* leaveth an inheritance to his children's children: and the wealth of the sinner *is* laid up for the just."

1 Corinthians 7:2 (KJV)

Nevertheless, *to avoid* fornication, let every man have his own wife, and let every woman have her own husband."

CHAPTER 7

1 John 4:18 (KJV)

"There is no fear in love; but perfect love casteth out fear: because fear hath torment. He that feareth is not made perfect in love."

Luke 12:48 (KJV)

But he that knew not, and did commit things worthy of stripes, shall be beaten with few *stripes*. For unto whomsoever much is given, of him shall be much required: and to whom men have committed much, of him they will ask the more."

Philippians 4:7 (KJV)

"And the peace of God, which passeth all understanding, shall keep your hearts and minds through Christ Jesus."

Galatians 5:22-23 (KJV)

"But the fruit of the Spirit is love, joy, peace, longsuffering, gentleness, goodness, faith,"

James 2:19 (KJV)

"Thou believest that there is one God; thou doest well: the devils also believe, and tremble."

CHAPTER 8

Genesis 2:18 (KJV)

"And the LORD God said, *It is* not good that the man should be alone; I will make him an help meet for him."

Ephesians 6:1 (KJV)

Children, obey your parents in the Lord: for this is right."

Ephesians 6:12 (KJV)

For we wrestle not against flesh and blood, but against principalities, against powers, against the rulers of the darkness of this world, against spiritual wickedness in high *places*."

Luke 12:47 (KJV)

And that servant, which knew his lord's will, and prepared not *himself*, neither did according to his will, shall be beaten with many *stripes*."

Exodus 3:14 (KJV)

And God said unto Moses, I AM THAT I AM: and he said, Thus shalt thou say unto the children of Israel, I AM hath sent me unto you."

CHAPTER 9

Genesis 3:15 (KJV)

And I will put enmity between thee and the woman, and between thy seed and her seed; it shall bruise thy head, and thou shalt bruise his heel."

Ephesians 6:18 (KJV)

Praying always with all prayer and supplication in the Spirit, and watching thereunto with all perseverance and supplication for all saints

CHAPTER 10

Proverbs 18:22 (KJV)

Whoso findeth a wife findeth a good *thing*, and obtaineth favour of the LORD."

Luke 12:47 (KJV)

"And that servant, which knew his lord's will, and prepared not *himself*, neither did according to his will, shall be beaten with many *stripes*."

HISTORY OF PRAYER

Jeremiah 9: 17-18 (KJV)

"Thus saith the LORD of hosts, Consider ye, and call for the mourning women, that they may come; and send for cunning *women*, that they may come:"

John 3:16 (KJV)

For God so loved the world, that he gave his only begotten Son, that whosoever believeth in him should not perish, but have everlasting life."

1 Thessalonians 5:17 (KJV)

"Pray without ceasing."

RESOURCES

http://docsouth.unc.edu/neh/bradford/summary

http://www.christianitytoday.com/history/issues/issue-33/secret-religion-of-slaves

http://www.ebwu.org/index.php/en/day-of-prayer

http://www.wicc.org/world-day-of-prayer/history-prayer/

http://nvdatabase.swarthmore.edu/content/liberian-women-act-end-civil-war-2003

ABOUT THE AUTHOR
DaVetta "Dee" Collins

As a Spiritual Leader, Coach, Speaker and Mentor, Dee had no aspirations of becoming a Publisher. In 2002, Dee's life took a major turn which divinely positioned her into media and publishing as an aid to bring healing to the hearts of people through radio, television, magazines, and events. As a result, Dee established Dunamis Woman Media & Publishing, Inc., a subsidiary of Dunamis Woman Enterprise LLC to take her vision to the next level. In 2012, her heart was passionately ignited to write and publish her first book, How to Pray with Power on Purpose.

During her journey, Dee has discovered that her mission and purpose for life is to speak truth through media as well as publish the heart of men and women across the globe willing to pursue healing in order to experience greatness. Dee's primary cause is to bring emotional healing to those who are sick and tired of being sick and tired and are willing to break through the barriers in their own mind for greater success.

As a serial entrepreneur, Dee currently reaches the masses and provides opportunities through mentorship and leadership development within her conglomerate of business entities: Dunamis Woman Enterprise LLC; Dunamis Woman Media & Publishing, Inc., and Impact & Inspire d/b/a Dee Speaks...You Think!, Dunamis Community Advocate Services; Dunamis Woman, Inc. and Dunamis Woman and Real Awesome Men (R.A.M.) Magazine, The Commercial Voice Real Estate Magazine, Next Level Leadership Media, and Dunamis Woman & R.A.M. International Ministries.

Dunamis Woman Media & Publishing, Inc.

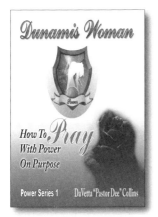

How to Pray with Power on Purpose
Power Series 1
DaVetta "Dee" Collins

Everyone Must Learn to Do It!
This book is a tool used to properly and rapidly equip you for the ministry of intercession. All of us are called to pray with power on purpose. Learning how to activate your power through prayer on purpose will challenge you in the area of your soul as well as empower you to confront and conquer aspects of yourself that attempts to keep you in bondage.

Real people willing to share their stories to expose, educate and empower others to break through barriers for great success are featured in this publication. Subscribe Today! Tell Your Story!

To order other books and magazines
published by
Dunamis Woman Media & Publishing, Inc.
or for more information
about the services provided
visit www.dunamis-woman.com